The Daily Telegraph

Digger's Diary

Tales from the Allotment

Victor Osborne

Illustrations by
Christopher Wormell

AURUM PRESS

This book is based on events and characters real and imagined.

First published in Great Britain
2000 by Aurum Press Ltd
25 Bedford Avenue, London WC1B 3AT

Text copyright © 2000 Victor Osborne
Illustrations copyright © 2000 Christopher Wormell

A catalogue record for this book is available from the British Library.

ISBN 1 85410 723 2

1 3 5 7 9 10 8 6 4 2
2000 2002 2004 2003 2001

Design by Roger Lightfoot
Printed and bound in Great Britain by
MPG Books Ltd, Bodmin

Contents

Acknowledgements

I would like to thank my wife, Harriet, and sons, Rupert and Giles, for enthusiastically eating what I grow and even occasionally helping on the plot. I am most grateful to Susannah Charlton, manager of Telegraph Books, who was instrumental in bringing this book about, for her advice and unfailing cheerfulness during the writing of it. Above all, I owe a great debt of gratitude to my fellow allotmenteers, too numerous to mention by name, who are endlessly helpful, kind and stimulating. No writer could have had a better inspiration for a book. Thank you all.

In memory of my father, Vic,
who first put a trowel and a packet of seeds into my hand

Digger's Diary

Introduction

One of my earliest childhood memories is of standing on my grandfather's allotment in a state of wonder at the clusters of fruit which surrounded me. It was a hot summer day, and while my father and grandfather discussed some serious matter or other, I wandered off into a secluded lane between the raspberries, currants and dwarf plums, picking and eating as I went and smearing myself with juice. For a two- or three-year-old boy it was better than having the free run of a sweet shop, because the allotment combined the pleasure of cramming my mouth full of fruit with the adventure of exploring a treasure island. I remember the peacefulness of it, and the sleepy hum of insects and the delicious smells of crushed fruit.

That was where my love affair with allotments began, and though it was to be another thirty years before I took on the first plot of my own, it was already in the blood. Both my grandfathers had cultivated allotments, virtually at opposite ends of England. My father's father had his plot in Tooting, South London, and my mother's father had one in Aspatria, Cumbria, nearly 350 miles away and where I lived for the early part of my life.

In the harsher economic times in which my grandfathers lived, their allotments were an essential source of extra food for their families. When I had a family of my own and decided to take an allotment, food was plentiful and cheap and growing it myself was almost incidental. I began the allotment principally as a form of therapy, an antidote to a working life spent chained to a desk with scores of others in a room with blinds drawn over the windows to exclude daylight in case it caused glare on computer screens. I commuted on crowded trains where I nearly always had to stand, in winter leaving home and returning in the dark. Long working days left me exhausted and in poor physical shape because my unhealthy, battery-hen existence was depriving me of wholesome activity and fresh air.

By chance, my first allotment, in Clapham, was only about a mile from where my grandfather's had been. It was overgrown and the soil was such heavy clay that it broke two hired mechanical cultivators. It was extremely hard work and I made every mistake a novice could make, but I loved every minute of it. My next allotment was in the grounds of a rectory and a much more responsive piece of land. I took my present allotment in Ealing, West London, in 1992. It is on a huge site which had originally been the orchards of a large private estate. The estate turned it over to allotments in the late nineteenth century.

The idea for the 'Digger's Diary' column came to me when I tried to find advice on cultivating allotments in newspapers and magazines and discovered that it was an area of gardening which was completely ignored at that time. Many other people must have been seeking similar advice, and I thought that if no one else was providing it, I should do so myself. Although no longer a novice, I was acutely aware that I was still making mistakes and that gardening was a learning process with no end to it. So rather than write a column of conventional advice, the disheartening sort which always reminds you of your shortcomings by telling you what you should have done, I decided to record the ups and downs of 'real' gardening, where the unexpected happens and things do go wrong. I also wanted to write about real gardeners and the rich and colourful culture of the people who cultivate allotments. In their sturdy independence and love of the soil and its green growing things, they are a living link with an ancient world which was governed by natural events and the slow turning of the seasons.

There is an extraordinary mixture of people on my site, of all ages and backgrounds. From my plot I can see allotmenteers who come from the United States, Ireland, The Netherlands, Belgium, Germany, France, Poland, Italy, Greece, Egypt, China, Korea, India, Africa and the Caribbean, all bound together harmoniously by the common purpose and language of gardening.

Growing my own food might have been incidental in the beginning, but that changed in the first season. The taste of home-grown fruit and vegetables, even humble things like potatoes and carrots, was a revelation equal to my childhood discovery of treasure island. My conversion to organic principles was a logical step on from that. If home-grown food tasted good, it would be even better without being drenched in chemicals, as well as healthier. The losses to pests and disease from not using chemicals was surprisingly small, though in any case most allotments can produce so much food that some loss is unimportant.

I have a whole shelf full of gardening books, but there is one I turn to so often it has become my bible, and its author my hero. It is *Your Garden Week By Week* by Arthur Hellyer, which has gone through countless editions since it was first published in 1936. It is a tribute to a great gardener, and the simple, clear and ungimmicky way in which Arthur wrote, that the advice he set down a lifetime ago is still wholly relevant today. Another influence, not always helpful, is my Inner Saxon Peasant, the ancestor who first tilled the soil and put a love of it into my blood. He is given to impulsive behaviour, petty envies and primitive solutions to problems. If he had his way, I would have a pig on the allotment to eat the couch grass and bindweed.

This book is dedicated to all allotmenteers, wherever they might be. May the sun always shine on your blessed plot of land and your cabbages be fit for kings.

January

New Year's Day

A quick trip to the allotment on the pretext of collecting sprouts for dinner, but really I need a good blast of fresh air to clear my hangover. It is a short walk through deserted suburban streets to the site. The gate is stiff from cold or rust and opens with a theatrical groan as if I am entering the graveyard where Boris Karloff is about to come back from the dead. In my fragile state, that thought does not strike me as at all fanciful. Even less so when I look at the Ruritanian scene in front of me.

I lock the gate in accordance with the shrill notices on it which say 'Keep the Vandals and Thieves Out Or Else', and stop for a moment to feel the change in atmosphere. I have crossed a frontier.

Behind lies the neatness and uniformity of suburban civilisation, with its identical houses and orderly gardens. In front is a wild landscape of unkempt vegetation and higgledy-piggledy sheds mostly built from salvaged timber and plastic and in various stages of collapse. The air feels and smells different. I sniff wood smoke and rotting leaves and the rankness of a fox, but more than that, a certain enticing rawness which warns me that things here are not as they are back there.

'Here There Be Tygers.'

The pause is brief. It is a bitterly cold day with a wind from the east which always brings the hardest weather. Streamers of white cloud cross a brilliant blue sky, and in mid-afternoon the sun is already sliding like a knob of melting butter towards the horizon. It will be dark soon.

There are four gateways into the site, and this one, the north gate, is large enough for a lorry to get through to an apron of land to deliver manure and wood chip or remove rubbish. To either side a broad track runs parallel with the fence, and I take the turning to the left. It is a huge site of more than 11 acres, with no discernible plan to it. The track seems to offer the only way around, but there is a network of tiny paths threading between the allotments which are only apparent when you are on one of them. You have to know where they are, like the secret tracks in a jungle or across a swamp.

The track divides and I take the right fork running across to the railway line which forms the southern boundary of the site. It was originally wide enough for a horse-drawn cart but can now barely take a wheelbarrow because the allotments have eaten away at it. I call it the Ridgeway as it is nearly 2 feet higher than the land it cuts through. I suppose that more than a century of intensive cultivation with the constant removal of soil on crops has lowered the surrounding land.

My plot is more or less in the middle of the site. It feels remote and peaceful there, far away from the sound of traffic. I always pause when I reach it to give the plot a quick survey. A glance will show what crops are coming into flower, which ones are wilting for lack of water and which are yellowing with disease.

There are few crops to see today or to obstruct the view over the land to the west and the tall tower of St Jude's Church, where pigeons are circling before roosting. The sky behind the tower is a burnt orange where the sun is setting. From where I stand the allotments appear to be as deserted as the nearby streets. I can see no one, but people are out there, probably quite a lot. The wisps of smoke from bonfires give some away. One or two are burning Christmas trees and the pine smell helps to clear my head.

The Brussels sprouts have been savaged by the pigeons, pecked in the middle so that they are open like roses, good for nothing now but the compost. I fetch a fork from the shed to lift some parsnips instead, but the ground is like iron and it won't go in. Cut some broccoli. The low rays of the sun glitter off specks of ice on the soil and I suddenly feel very cold and eager to be beside the log fire at home.

On the way back to the gate I pass the Birdman's plot just as the door of his bungalow-like shed opens to let out a soft yellow light. 'Hey,' he calls to me. 'Come along in and have a glass of something to welcome the New Year.' Inside, the shed is comfortable and heated with a gas fire. There is a carpet on the floor, upholstered armchairs, a gas cooker, oil lamps and a television set running off a car battery. An old dresser holds drawers full of seeds, and dried bunches of herbs hang from the ceiling. The walls are lined with cages which hold rabbits and birds, mostly canaries and budgerigars. Outside there are smaller sheds for pigeons, hens and ducks.

'What'll you have?' he asks in a bright Irish accent, clinking bottles. His wife, Molly, says in a softer Scots accent: 'Happy New Year,' and smiles sweetly at me and nods her head. She is drinking tea.

'Tea,' I say, the thought of anything alcoholic causing my head to throb again.

'Get away,' he says in disbelief, a bottle of Irish whiskey hovering over a beer glass.

'Really.'

'That's just fine,' says Molly and pours me a cup from the teapot. I sit down.

'Too much last night?' he says, and laughs when I nod.

Every time I go into their shed I am amazed by it. I feel I have walked into a place described in a children's story by Arthur Ransome or Robert Louis Stevenson. It is at once unreal and very familiar. It is also very warm and in no time I am feeling drowsy. I could go to sleep here and sail away with the Swallows and Amazons, or Long John Silver. I drain the cup and with difficulty rouse myself and go on my way. Outside, night is falling and the stars sparkle like chips of ice.

So, there are no sprouts or parsnips to go with the leg of pork from a pig reared by friends on a Welsh smallholding, but there is broccoli and, from the freezer, home-grown French and runner beans, potatoes, carrots, and my own apple sauce.

Apple Sauce

A Bramley is best for this. Peel, cut into quarters, core and slice thinly. Put in pan with 3 tablespoons of cider instead of water if for pork, add the zest of half a lemon, a knob of butter and sugar to taste, simmer until soft and serve hot or cold with a sprinkling of nutmeg.

Afterwards, the last of the frozen raspberries. I watch my wife and sons eating what I have grown with a keen appetite and say nothing, but feel a great sense of achievement. It is enormously satisfying to be able to grow wholesome food and put it on the table. Is that why I took on an allotment? Probably, but I am too full and sleepy to think about it.

Saturday

Fred intercepts me as I come out of the gate at lunchtime after taking a bag of vegetable peelings and mouldy bread to the compost. He has a house nearby and had an allotment himself once, just over the boundary from his garden. He gave it up because it wasn't far enough away. His wife could still summon him from over the fence.

He invites me to watch the rugby with him, and a few minutes later we are in the Fox and Ferret raising pints of beer with the game about to start on the television in the corner. The pub is conveniently placed outside the east gates of the allotment site and opposite St Jude's Church and its adjoining hall, where the Allotment Association holds its annual show and other formal meetings. It should be called the Holy Trinity because of the neat proximity of church, pub and hall.

'Is there a lot of hanky-panky on the allotments?' asks Fred.

The question baffles me. 'What?'

'You know. Sex.'

'Sex?' I am slow on the uptake because the question has turned my mind to innocent thoughts of bees and the pollination of flowers.

'Yes. Late at night I see lights on down there. In sheds. What else can it be?'

I lower my glass to the bar while I consider this. It seems ridiculous. I have to admit to myself reluctantly that allotmenteers, in their muddy boots and sensible clothes and usually solitary souls, are not the sexiest of people. 'No,' I say dismissively. 'On the allotments? It's far too cold.'

'It's a good way to get warm though, isn't it,' he says and laughs. A roar from the television signals that England has scored a try. Could he be right? Are the allotments a hotbed of seething passions which I have never noticed before? The crowd groans as England botches the conversion, but my attention has been fatally distracted. Then I think of someone.

'Of course, there is Erogenous Jones.'

'Oh, yes,' says Fred. We look at one another. Erogenous – real name Roger – Jones is a notorious ladies' man. I have often wondered how he found the time to cultivate an allotment. Could it be just a cover for his amorous activities?

Digger's Diary

Sunday
Down to the Trading Hut just before it closes at noon to order
seed potatoes and onion sets. I should have put my order in last
October but forgot. The Trading Hut is an ugly industrial building of concrete panels and corrugated iron tucked into a corner
by the railway line and to the left of the east gate. It is a regular
target for paint-spraying vandals and the only building I know
whose appearance is actually improved by graffiti.

The Hut is open on Saturdays and Sunday mornings. It is
staffed by volunteers and sells reduced-price tools, seeds, fertiliser, potting compost, bamboo canes, netting, and a hundred
other things. It carries a large range of pesticides and similar
toxic chemicals. The organic revolution has an uphill struggle
here. It is also the place to go to catch up on gossip and seek
advice on gardening problems. If no one there at the time knows
the solution they will know somebody who does.

The Jam Queen is on duty today with the other Ladies of the
Hut. That's good. I can usually charm a cup of tea out of her
and sometimes a slice of home-made cake.

'Hello, darling,' she says breaking into a huge smile which
sends her glasses slipping towards the tip of her nose. 'Tea's finished, but try a bit of this.' She takes the lid off a tin and offers
me a slice of Victoria sponge, as yellow as butter, with a thick red
stripe of raspberry jam though the middle. I can smell it from 6
feet away. It dissolves in the mouth like a souffle and the filling
tastes as if the berries have just been picked from the canes.

At the autumn show last year, I beat her to first place in the
jam section with my blackcurrant jam. I have felt vaguely guilty
about that ever since, as I only made it because I couldn't think
what else to do with a bumper crop of fat and juicy blackcurrants. I was a first-time-lucky amateur stealing the glory from a
skilled professional. Far from putting her nose out, my win tick-
led her enormously, and she tests her new recipes on me.

'That's a seedless one. Don't ask me how I got the pips out or
I'll tell you.' She gives a smoker's laugh which is a cross between
a cough and a cackle. 'What do you think?' The three other

10

Ladies crane forward to study me closely as I bite into it and crumbs fall on to my jacket.

'Queeny, what can I say? It's delicious,' and I kiss my finger-tips, hoping there may be a second slice in the tin. The Ladies relax and smile approvingly. I feel that I have passed some sort of test and become an honorary Jam Lady, which is very pleasing.

The Hon. Sec. bustles through the door as I enquire about the potatoes. 'You've left that a bit late, Victor,' he butts in. 'I put notices up in September about it and mentioned it in the October newsletter. You must get organised.'

He is a local councillor and keen on organisation. He has enormous energy, and since he became the Hon. Sec. last year he has transformed the Allotment Association, invigorating it with new ideas and purpose and bringing on new people. Someone half-jokingly said that he had halved the average age of the committee from eighty to forty. He thought up the idea of having summer parties in members' gardens with an entry charge and using the money to finance a winter programme of gardening lectures by experts in the chuch hall. The parties have been so successful that there is money left over and he is talking about buying equipment like mechanical cultivators and shredders to be loaned out.

Queeny sees my crestfallen expression and shakes her head sympathetically. 'We sent the order off to the supplier weeks ago. Did you want a lot?'

'No, just 3 kilos of Charlotte.' They are a second early potato, waxy and oval, which I tried for the first time last year, and they were magnificent on flavour, texture and pest resistance. By far the best I have ever grown, better even than Pink Fir Apple. They can be lifted as soon as first earlies, but some can be left in the ground longer to grow as big as a main crop.

'We can probably manage something for you,' says the Hon. Sec.

'Thanks,' I say, and add hopefully: 'Onion sets?'

He snorts. 'Excuse me, but I have just walked past your plot and it is still covered in weeds from last year. If you haven't done any digging, where are you going to plant them? Some people are putting theirs in already. Mind, I think it's a bit early for onions, but I planted shallots last month. They should be put in on the shortest day and harvested on the longest.'

'Well . . .' What I want to say is: 'How do you manage to make me feel like a backsliding schoolboy?' but instead I say guiltily: 'I'm going to start digging as soon as the weather gets better.'

'Right.' He nods and bustles off to see about a bulk order of manure.

'Don't worry, darling,' says Queeny. 'We've stopped taking individual orders for onion sets. We buy them by the sackful now, so there'll be plenty for you.'

As I walk the short distance up the slope to my plot, I notice the weather has got better. It is not nearly as cold as it was. The wind is in my face, from the south-west where the rain comes from, and is not warm exactly, but soft. Grey clouds are scudding overhead. A good downpour will soften the ground nicely. I prefer to dig after rain, even though the ground is heavier, because the soil is easier to work and turns over more neatly. When dry, it is light, almost sandy, and doesn't bind together well.

The allotments have not shut down completely during this mild winter as they usually do. Some plants have continued to grow, including, surprisingly, the tender geraniums I forgot to lift in the autumn which are doing well in the shelter of the shed. Frosts have been light and the ground is relatively warm. There is already a foretaste of spring in the bright-yellow flowers of winter jasmine which cascade over several fences. I should not forget, though, that February sometimes produces the coldest weather here.

Cut spears of broccoli, a cabbage and fork up some parsnips. They are poor specimens, all shoulder and no body with a thin root. I can tell just by looking at them that they will be woody and hardly worth cooking. Take a decision not to grow them again.

Thursday

It rained for three days, so now I must dig. Nearly all allotments are long and fairly narrow, with public paths on either side and at top and bottom separating them from one another. Mine is different. It is square, with public paths on only two sides, the other two having hedges of blackberry, loganberry and blackthorn to mark the boundary with other plots. The shape and the hedges make the allotment feel more like a garden, more private. I have divided it into four square sub-plots, like a Battenberg cake, with my own grass paths between them, so I can work all areas from inside the allotment instead of from the outside paths.

The sub-plots aren't exactly square and they are not all the same size. On one is the shed and an unfinished tool locker, which holds bulky items that would clutter up the shed and that have a low value, so I can replace them easily if they are stolen. Bean poles, chicken wire, netting, sacks of plastic plant pots and various odds and ends which might come in useful one day.

On another are three wooden-framed compost bins, which are slowly disintegrating.

One of the sub-plots is devoted to permanent plants, mostly fruit. Raspberries, blackcurrants, redcurrants, gooseberries, rhubarb, asparagus, comfrey and rosemary. The others are cultivated on a three-year rotation plan which varies from year to year, though essentially it is potatoes and other root crops followed by beans, peas and sweetcorn, followed by onions, split with cabbages and broccoli. Salads are fitted in wherever there is a gap.

Still smarting from the Hon. Sec.'s rebuke, I make a start with the onion bed, digging over the square which still holds the brown and twisted stalks of last year's runner and French beans. Their roots should be left in the ground because, as they decay, they release nitrogen for the next crop. Leafy plants like cabbages and other brassicas benefit most from nitrogen so I will leave space for them.

I make good progress for about two hours, but in my desire to make up for lost time I am going too fast. The soil is heavy with water. I ignore the twinges from my lower back as long as I can, then there is a sharp stab of pain and I straighten up with a grimace, clutching at it.

'You too?' calls Chicken Tom, putting down the wheelbarrow he is trundling past on the Ridgeway. 'Last week mine went as I was leaning over the workbench to pick up a spanner.' He mimes the sudden freeze of a back sufferer realising a split second too late that he is in trouble. 'Just like that. I was in bed for two days, unable to move.'

My smile is as stiff as my back as I ask how he made such an amazing recovery that he is able to push that huge pile of manure. He waves a hand in the air and says vaguely: 'The secret is the right posture.'

Chicken Tom got his name because he will only eat chickens that he has raised himself on a wholesome diet of untreated corn. He believes that supermarket chicken is full of food additives which will make him ill or impotent. He has a large hen house on his allotment and a secluded spot behind it where he slaughters and plucks them. By contrast, the Birdman and Molly treat their birds as pets. They eat the eggs but would never dream of eating the chickens or ducks.

I decide to call it a day. My back is stiffening up and the wind has gone round to the north; it is getting colder by the minute.

Friday
I can't bend to tie my shoelaces. Outside, gritty snow is falling and being whipped away by the wind before it can settle. Give the plot a miss and get on with other things which require no bending or lifting. After supper I get one of my boys to fetch more coal before he starts his homework and settle down by the fire with my feet on a stool to ease my back. Beside me on the sofa is a pile of seed catalogues and on my lap a notebook and pencil. I pick up the first catalogue and, before opening it, pause to relish the moment. I am supposed to be planning what I will

grow in the coming season, but this is where I slip into fantasy gardening. In the next hour, while my wife and children sit in the kitchen and leave me in peace, I will mentally roam an allotment that has become a sub-tropical Garden of Eden where everything grows without effort, and the tomatoes are the size of melons and the melons the size of pumpkins.

First, I look to see what Arthur was up to in January 1936. He was already sprouting, or chitting, his potatoes and thinking of planting some early in large pots, and sowing onions, carrots, tomatoes and leeks indoors. He even suggests starting off French beans in a greenhouse for an early crop in May. Goodness. I often don't even get round to planting them till May. Must get cracking.

Monday

My back is better, but I don't want to risk it seizing up again. The temperature is only just above freezing and I have a theory that overexertion is more likely to cause muscle damage when the weather is very cold. Whether it is true or not, it is a good excuse not to go out on a miserable day like today. Switch on all the kitchen lights to shut out the grey pallor of a winter's afternoon and spread the seed catalogues on the table. I must make a determined effort to draw up a proper and sensible list of crops to grow. An image comes to mind of a palm tree waving above the turquoise blue of the Caribbean and I sternly shove it out of the way. To business. No more fantasies. I am already too far behind in everything.

Divide a sheet of paper into four to represent my sub-plots and number them, then shade in the shed, compost bins and other unusable areas. Number one is onions because that is the first crop to go in. Actually, it's not. I planted garlic back in September and October, but I'll overlook that for now. The catalogues offer a wide variety and I make a choice based on flavour – strongish; size – largeish; and keeping qualities – longish.

A non-gardening friend once looked at the net bags of onions hanging from the rafters in the garage and asked why I bothered to grow so much of something which was so cheap to buy. I tried to explain that anything home-grown tastes enormously better than stuff from supermarkets, and the improvement in flavour is most marked in the humblest of vegetables: onions, potatoes, carrots and cabbages. But more than that, onions are easy to grow, requiring no attention apart from occasional weeding, and reliably producing a large crop. This is good for morale, particularly in years when drought, pests or disease have played havoc with everything else. It is quite possible by juggling autumn and spring plantings to grow all the onions a family can eat in a year from a relatively small piece of land.

'Oh,' she said, without conviction. Clearly not an onion lover, like me.

The choice is Stuttgart Giant and Red Baron as sets, which are baby onions whose development has been temporarily arrested, and seeds of Bedfordshire Champion, Fen Globe and the spring onion White Lisbon. To those I add sets of Pikant shallots. Sets are more dependable than seeds, doing away with the problems of poor germination and damping off, when seedlings suddenly collapse and die. Yet the odd thing is that the largest onions are grown from seed. They should be started now indoors, or even earlier, in December.

Stuttgart is an old-fashioned variety which is no longer offered by some catalogues. I have grown it for years because it is dependable in all weather conditions and the bulbs mature to a good cooking size of about half a pound and store well for six months or more. Red Baron is, well, red, with a mild flavour and looks and tastes good raw in salads. The other two are more temperamental. They could be very big, and I am growing them with an eye to the autumn show. The shallots are fiddly to peel, though worth it. They are lovely cooked whole in stews and have a better flavour than small onions when pickled.

Even with so many varieties to grow, there will be space on sub-plot number one for other things, though I can't decide what at the moment. I write 'What else?' in red ink on the square so that I don't forget.

Beans and peas move over onto sub-plot number two. This is easier, because I grew Scarlet Emperor runner beans and Viola Cornetti climbing French beans last year and they both did so well that I kept seed from them which I dried over the Aga and kept in the fridge in paper bags. Must check that they are O.K. and haven't gone damp and mouldy, or worse still, been thrown into a pot and eaten. This happened one year with a whole range of seeds when the Spanish au pair was rummaging around for something to cook. They included some decidedly dodgy things like lupins and nasturtiums. I'm surprised we weren't poisoned.

Beside Scarlet Emperor I write 'and something else' to compare taste, and after Viola Cornetti I add Blue Lake. This is another climbing French bean and I grow them in that form instead of as bushes because they produce a bigger crop, out of reach of slugs and easier to pick. Then a row of broad beans. They should have been started last November to get an early crop, though they can be sown as late as April.

Next, a row each of sugar snap peas and mange-tout, and a big block of sweetcorn. That will fill sub-plot two, because the shed and tool locker take up a lot of space, and I must also find room for home-made cold-frames for raising seedlings of tomato, pepper and lettuce. They will go beside the shed, though for now they are still just a collection of wooden-framed windows rescued from skips which are stacked against one side of it; I will knock them together one day soon.

Sub-plot three will be potatoes, carrots, and possibly leeks. Sub-plot four is already filled with fruit bushes. I will have to find a home for all the other things I want grow, including lettuce, radish, courgettes and various herbs. For now, I just list them in the margin.

I sit back and look at the plan with satisfaction before filling out the order forms. It makes me think, even more than the digging, that spring is around the corner and that I have a map to guide me into the season. The start of a new gardening season is like the start of a love affair. Whatever happened last time in the way of disasters and unfulfilled hopes is forgotten. Everything will be different this time. The possibilities are limitless.

Wednesday
On the way to continue the digging I stop by Poppy and Carlo's plot to admire the blue bottles which have been dropped over the tops of tall bamboo canes and sway in the wind like a dynamic sculpture. This allotment is unlike any other I have ever seen and is a constant source of delight. It is also deeply subversive.

Poppy has rejected most of the cardinal rules of traditional allotmenteering, and many old-timers must wince at the sight of it. Her plot is a great swirl of flowing colours and textures, like an Impressionist painting. It is impossible to tell at first glance where the vegetables are, or indeed if there are any. There are no straight lines, no angular beds for individual crops, no patches of bare earth. Vegetables, flowers and shrubs are mixed together according to how they set one another off. They are allowed to go to seed if they add a special decorative quality, and there are some magnificent purple balls of onion seedheads on tall stems. Some areas are edged with wine bottles, bottoms up. A wooden owl perches on a weathered beam, the plastic arm and hand of a shop-window mannequin emerges from the ground as if it belongs to a Greek earth nymph, and an ancient bentwood coatstand, painted bright red, keeps an apple tree company. To achieve and maintain such an individual and artistic plot requires much more effort and time than a conventional one. Poppy sometimes starts work on it at six in the morning in summer.

Saturday
A lorry load of horse manure from a local stable has been dumped by the gates on a help-yourself basis. This stuff is like gold dust and half of it is gone by the time I find out, and the rest will go by lunchtime. Speed is essential and I try to cajole my youngest into helping, but he gives me a teenage sneer.

'All right, how much?' I say, giving in to market forces.

'Five pounds,' he replies as if he's doing me a big favour.

'What?' I cry in outrage, and consider listing all the things I used to do for my father without reward, but I know it will just confirm his opinion that I am a soft touch. We settle on 30 pence per barrowload and get to work.

Saleem, another of my neighbours, is hard at it and he advises me to spread the manure on the ground like a carpet so the rain will wash the heat out of it. By heat, he means the fresh chemicals from the horses which will scorch plants. Most gardeners reckon stable manure needs up to a year in a compost heap before it is fit to use, so spreading it now may risk damage to young plants growing through it in the spring.

Saleem dismisses that anxiety. 'It will be all right. Just scrape it to one side when you put seedlings in. The big advantage is that the manure will stop weeds from growing.'

It is bitterly cold again, with flurries of snow and after an hour the boy and I have had enough. We have shifted a dozen barrowloads, which is not bad.

Tuesday

The only person in sight is the Birdman. He has backed his van through the gates and is unloading a couple of elegant Edwardian wardrobes he got for next to nothing from a house-clearance sale. He will turn them into nesting boxes. He invites me to admire the grain in the wood, which is a delightfully light, almost rosy, mahogany. I hope the hens appreciate it.

The temperature last night was –5 degrees Centrigrade, and the ice in the water troughs is 6 inches thick. What has happened to the mild and damp winters that global warming was supposed to have produced in the last few years? At least the cold will kill off those annoying pests which have survived the warmer winters. It is a bit of a shock to find the white fly in the Brussels sprouts are still alive and active. How much cold can they stand?

On the way to the gate I pass Mad Alice bent over an open cold-frame where she is potting up cuttings of chrysanthemums. No one calls her Mad Alice to her face – they wouldn't dare. Her temper and sharp language are notorious. She likes to be called Mrs Springs, though she never mentions a Mr Springs, and claims that Alice Springs in Australia was named after her. Nobody has had the courage to ask her why. She is dressed in a tattered overcoat, turned-down Wellington boots and a dis-integrating straw hat lashed down with a scarf. She may be mad and unhygienic, but she grows the best chrysanthemums and dahlias in the district.

'Afternoon,' I say brightly. She jumps and turns on me.

'Don't creep up on people and startle them like that,' she scolds. 'You could have given me one of my turns.'

'Sorry.' Smile apologetically and hurry on.

Friday

The first of the seed orders arrives in the post. Rush off to the garden centre to buy a large bag of seed compost, then get the trays out of the garage, wash them and start sowing. Soak the larger seed, like peas and broad beans, in warm water for a few hours to speed up germination. Do the same with the sweet peas, but first scratch the hard shells against a matchbox to make it easier for them to absorb water. Still too early to sow the rest of the beans and sweetcorn.

To the church hall after supper for a lecture on Kew Gardens by one of its managers. The subject is Soil Management and Biological Interaction, which sounds heavy, but the lecturer turns out to be a keen allotmenteer who is laying out trial allotments at Kew. I goggle at the slides which show a series of huge compost heaps like a mountain range. They are so big they have to be turned by J.C.B.s and constantly watered, probably to stop them getting so hot they catch fire. Glad to hear him say that soil should be kept covered in winter to prevent damage to its structure, even if this means leaving it unweeded. Afterwards, across the road to the Fox and Ferret.

Sunday
Much warmer and sunny. The six children who walk past my plot look so wholesome and purposeful that they make me smile. They are neatly dressed in bright clothes and walk silently in single file in descending order of age and height, the oldest no more than twelve and the youngest about six. They are well behaved with that self-absorbed earnestness of children lost in some innocent game of adventure and imagination. I glance back the way they have come, half expecting to see that they have just walked off the film set for a breakfast-cereal or washing-powder commercial.

Still smiling I greet them: 'Hi, kids. Where are you off to?'

The leader says: 'To help my aunty. Over there.' He waves vaguely. Great, I think, returning to the digging. Get them started young.

A couple of minutes later there is the sound of breaking glass, followed by childish laughter and whooping. The children are running across plots throwing bricks into greenhouses and cold-frames, pulling up plants and canes and overturning compost bins. It is an orgy of mindless destruction and they are enjoying themselves enormously.

I fetch the Manager from his plot some distance away, and when they see us coming, the children split into two groups as if this is a well-practised manoeuvre. One group seems to melt through the fence along the railway cutting and the other shins over the main gates untroubled by the three strands of barbed wire along the top. Safely on the other side, the leader, still looking wholesome and angelic, gives me a mouthful of some the foulest language I have heard. Incensed, I start forward. I have always wanted to make a citizen's arrest, and this seems the perfect opportunity. An open-and-shut case if ever there was one.

'Don't,' says the Manager, putting out a restraining hand.

'Why not?' I ask, reaching for the key to unlock the gates. The boy has taken a step back but remains defiant and cocky.

'The police say we cannot touch them.'

I turn to the Manager in disbelief. 'What?'

'Lay a hand on one of them and when the police come, they will arrest you for assaulting a child.'

'You must be joking,' I say.

'No, I'm not,' he replies grimly. 'All we can do is try to frighten them away.'

Stunned, I watch the children swagger off down the road, taking their time and swearing at two women who come out of their houses to ask what all the fuss is about. The youngest are probably not even able to tie their own shoelaces yet. But they know how to smash up other people's property and they know they are untouchable, which is why they vandalised the place in broad daylight in full view of a score of people.

Hearing about this in the Hut later, Brutally Frank says, 'There is only thing to do to kids like that, to be brutally frank. I would tie them on to the fence, tell them the crows will come and peck their eyes out and leave them to sweat for half an hour. That'd stop them.'

February

Tuesday

The postman delivers a booklet from the local council with the title 'Kitchen Composting Scheme', followed by the question: 'Could you give a composter a good home?' None better. Although I have three home-made bins, I don't like to put kitchen waste in them because they are open – cooked food attracts rats and foxes. And because they are open, it takes about a year for the contents to rot down. A closed plastic bin works much more quickly.

The booklet says that to encourage households to compost their kitchen waste the council is offering 2000 compost bins at the giveaway price of £5. In return, each recipient will be asked to fill in a chart recording what goes into their bin over a year.

There are four types to choose from: a wormery and three enclosed plastic bins of different sizes. This is a real bargain. I know that the average cost of a composter is about £45, having priced bins in a garden centre before Christmas and decided that they were too expensive for the children to buy me one as a present.

I want them all, especially the one called the Hotter Rotter – is this inspired by Erogenous Jones? I ring the council and explain to a lady in Environmental Services why I need a full set. She sniffily says that one is the limit per household. I point out that if I put one on each of my four sub-plots, I could provide the council with a useful comparison of how the different types work. She is not impressed, and replies that they are intended for gardens, not allotments, and rings off. I get the impression that the whole idea of wormeries and compost is deeply distasteful to her and she really belongs in some more genteel department, like Libraries.

If I can only have one, which will it be? I like the idea of hundreds of worms busily chewing up my rubbish, but reluctantly decide against them. Friends who have them say they are temperamental and have a habit of dying off, and even when everything goes smoothly, they produce mostly liquid and only a small amount of solid compost. Even more reluctantly, I decide the Hotter Rotter is too small to do the job – sorry, Erogenous – and plump for the biggest of them all, the Soil Saver, which has a capacity of 350 litres, which is an odd way to measure compost. I post the application form with a cheque on the way to the plot.

After a night of rain the earth is heavy, and digging the last of the onion bed brings on twinges in my back, especially when I bend to lift the loaded spade. The other evening there was a programme on television about the restoration of a Victorian country-house garden in Cornwall and I watched spellbound as three gardeners using spades with handles as tall as themselves

24

turned the soil without bending at all. They made digging look effortless, almost pleasurable, and worked much faster than any diggers I know using a normal spade. I have been to three garden centres since in search of a long-handled one but none of the staff had a clue what I was talking about, so maybe the spades were as Victorian as the garden and are no longer made.

Wednesday
The broad beans, sugar snap peas and carrots have come through in the seed trays on the kitchen windowsill. I take it as a signal that the growing season has started, so grab the bags of onion and shallot sets and head off to the plot. Some people rake and smooth their onion beds until they have a fine tilth good enough for sowing a lawn. This might be of benefit for seeds, but I don't see the point if sets are going in. I do agree, though, that onions benefit from being planted into firm soil which their roots can grip, so I pin out the orange marker line and tread the soil down alongside it with my Wellington boots. Then I put a kneeling board on the ground to work from and push the sets in until only the tips are showing, and give them a half-twist to anchor them well. The blade of a trowel serves as a useful rough-and-ready spacer.

The Hon. Sec.'s faith in the old gardening wisdom that shallots should be planted on the shortest day of the year puzzles me. Putting anything into the ground in the depths of winter with the worst weather still to come seems to be asking for trouble. They will not start to grow until conditions improve and some of them are bound to rot in the cold, wet ground. I know the garlic will be sitting out through the winter, but that is different. It was planted in September and October, early enough to root and sprout and establish itself before winter checked its growth. Garlic actually benefits from a period of cold. Autumn-planted bulbs are always bigger and juicier than ones planted in the spring.

Two rows of shallots are followed by five of onions, and then a prickling on the neck tells me that I am not alone. Saleem and Alan are standing on the path behind me, watching.

'You shouldn't do that,' says Saleem.

'What?'

'Push the sets in. It damages the plate on the bottom from which the roots grow, and twisting makes the damage worse.' I turn one of the tiny bulbs over. There is a flat spot, not much bigger than a pinhead, on the bottom which I have never noticed before.

'Oh,' I say, rather taken aback. 'I have always planted them like that.'

'And have they always been slow to germinate because they are having to develop a second set of roots to replace the ones which have been scraped off?'

I hesitate while I think about it. Have I been abusing my onions all these years? Being soft-hearted, I like to think not, but I have to admit that I have often glanced enviously at the huge onions growing on Saleem's neighbouring plot and wondered what his secret was. His soil must be very similar to mine, yet mine produces very ordinary onions. He comes over and takes the set from my hand, picks up the trowel and prepares to demonstrate. He is a railway-maintenance engineer but his true vocation is clearly teaching.

'What you should do is dig a little hole.' He digs a little hole. 'And drop it in and firm the soil around it like that.' He takes another one and repeats the process, knowing that I am a slow learner. I stand up and step back in the hope that he will carry on down the row and give me a much-needed break.

Alan is another of my neighbours. He is about eighty and took on his plot before many of the current allotmenteers were born. Though he is frail and his hands are unsteady, he manages to come down most days when the weather is not too bad, and his plot is always well tended. He never offers advice unless asked for it, and then always gives it in a positive way. I ask if his onions are in yet.

'No. It's too early for me. I reckon that if the sets get a frost on them they'll go to seed later on and the bulbs won't be up to much.' Seeing the flicker of anxiety on my face, he adds reassuringly:

'You're putting yours in a sheltered spot, so they should be all right.'

'There you are,' says Saleem, straightening up and handing me back the trowel, while casting a critical eye over the plot. 'Where are your broad beans? They should be well up by now.'

'I wasn't going to grow any this year because the children won't eat them and they always get attacked by blackfly, but I changed my mind and put some in a few weeks ago.'

'They won't get blackfly if you start them off early enough, and spray them at the first sign of trouble.' We are all getting cold standing here and I decide this is not the time to explain that I cannot spray because I am organic in case it starts a lengthy debate.

I wasn't organic when I first took an allotment. I had a shelf full of chemicals and two sprayers and a watering can used exclusively for weedkiller. But my conversion was rapid. It seemed obvious that poisonous chemicals sprayed on anything I grew would linger in it to be eaten by me and my family. There was always enough of most crops so that anything truly rendered inedible by pests or disease could be discarded without causing a shortage. Then there was the succession of food scares caused by chemicals and other things to confirm my worst fears.

The actual point of my conversion came the day after I had covered the ground around some young plants with about half a kilo of slug pellets. They were a bright blue, with a sort of radioactive malevolence about them. I looked at this carpet of poison and realised that about 99 per cent of it would remain uneaten by slugs and be absorbed into the ground. What then?

The label might say that the toxic chemicals would be rendered harmless by the soil, but suddenly I did not believe it. I no longer wholly trusted agri-scientists. They had too long a record of getting things wrong or misleading people, going back through B.S.E. and organo-phospates to D.D.T. If chemicals from those pellets went into the soil, some of it was bound to be absorbed by my beans and cabbages and lettuce. It might not make me noticeably ill when I ate them, but it would not do me any good. And what about my children?

I put on a pair of heavy rubber gloves and picked up the pellets. It took more than an hour and I didn't get them all but I felt a sense of relief when I tipped them down the drain. Most of the other chemicals followed as I realised that spraying often had only a marginal effect on pests and the best defence was a healthy plant growing strongly. The first organic carrots served at home tasted as if they had come from a different planet from the ones sold in supermarkets.

I am not dogmatic about organic cultivation, and a couple of packets of chemicals still lurk at the back of the shed. The problem is that there is no organic treatment for bindweed, one of the banes of my life, and I am sometimes driven by weed rage to spray the couch grass on paths and other uncultivated areas. I am also aware that going organic can be a bit of a luxury. While I am prepared to lose a certain percentage of my crops to pests and diseases as the price of being organic, I know that most commercial growers cannot do the same without going out of business.

Thursday
About an inch of snow fell in the night. It will probably melt by evening. Drive to the allotments for a look. Snow blankets everything except the sheds and greenhouses and they have lost their sharp edges and decrepit appearance and become things of mystery. No one in sight and nothing moves, though a fox's tracks pass the Birdman's hen house in a single-minded straight line. A dog's tracks would wander all over the place. The music from the film of *The Snowman* comes to mind. The allotments look quite magical and other-worldly. Decide not to open the gates and go in because my footsteps would spoil the fairy-tale look of the snow. Get back in the car and slip and slide away.

Monday
The snow did not clear until this morning, and a few tiny patches still linger in hollows. Look at onion sets and wonder

anxiously if Alan is right about frost. There have been four nights of it, and the ground is still a bit crunchy. February is often the coldest month, but I am always seduced by the sight of daffodils and buds swelling on fruit trees into expecting it to be warmer than it is. Try to pull carpet off the bed where the potatoes will go but it is as stiff as cardboard, so leave it.

As the soil is light and does not benefit from the action of frost breaking down clods, I dig patches of land only as I need them to put a crop in. The problem with that is if I am delayed by bad weather or laziness, I quickly get behind and start to panic. Now the onion bed is finished, I should be digging the ground for the potatoes which will go in next month.

Tuesday
The last of the seed orders has arrived. The packets are arranged in a cardboard shoe box in the order in which they should be planted. Some will be sown in a succession of small batches – lettuce, peas, radish – and nearly all of them will have enough seed left over to plant next year.

There are seed trays on windowsills all over the house. I am running out of space for them as I tend to put everything into trays, even those seeds which can be started off in the ground. This is to avoid the depredations of slugs and birds. Two years ago I lost three whole sowings of French beans, about 120 altogether. As soon as the tender green sprouts emerged from the ground they were eaten up. As space runs out I tell myself off for not building the cold-frames. A greenhouse would be even better.

Thursday
Off to join the other members of the local Organic Gardening Society, who I call the Orgies for short. They meet once a month in the Quaker Hall in winter, usually to hear an improving lecture on caring for wildlife, or pest control through companion planting. In summer they often take trips to interesting or unusual gardens, and I am still upset that I missed the one to the Roof Gardens in Kensington, West London (the gardens that

used to belong to Derry and Tom's department store), last August. It sounded brilliant, but I was away on holiday.

The Orgies are quite separate from the Allotment Association, and only a few of them are allotmenteers. Those who are have learnt to try to spread the organic message to their unconverted neighbours by example rather than by preaching. Allotmenteers are individualists who guard their independence and take a fierce pride in what they grow and how they grow it. To criticise their methods would be worse than criticising their children, and a surefire way of creating bitter enmities. The division between organic and chemical gardeners is still deep, which is surprising given the amount of public attention lavished on worries about food safety.

It is partly generational. Many gardeners who are middle-aged and older were brought up to believe that the only good bug was a dead bug, and that a poisonous spray was the quickest way of killing it. They possess a natural conservatism which is resistant to change, not surprising in such an ancient activity. If a particular way of doing things was good enough for their father or mother, it is good enough for them, and most of the time they are perfectly right. I still use techniques – and tools – that I saw my grandfather use.

The conservatism is reinforced by the traditional approach to planting, whereby all crops are arranged in blocks of related plants, and the blocks are arranged in rigid lines with precise spacing between plants to maximise production. Cabbages and onions and carrots standing to attention like guardsmen on parade and looking equally impressive, until a plant keels over here and there. Then the loss is immediately apparent in the ragged line and demands an instant remedy, and the only quick fix is a chemical one. But the loss of one or two plants does not matter, and only ever did in times of desperate hardship long ago. If planting conformity is ignored, the loss won't even be noticeable. Many organic plots are a jumble of vegetables and flowers; the untidiness may irritate the old-guard allotmenteers but it is a more relaxed way of doing things.

Tonight we have a speaker from the Friends of the Earth who is giving an update on Genetically Modified Organisms, or G.M.O.s. This is a subject which casts a long shadow. Allotmenteers find the scientific arguments for and against it just as baffling as everyone else. Because of their close connection with the soil they can readily see the advantages of plants which can defend themselves against attack by pests and disease, but many feel a deep anxiety that genetic engineering may involve a violation of nature which could have irreversible effects and be a price too high to pay for the benefits it may bring.

The elderly lady giving the talk refers frequently to a thick bundle of notes which seem to be in the wrong order. It does not matter because she is preaching to the converted, and in the long pauses while she searches for the right bits of paper, members of the audience tell each other about the latest G.M. scares and scandals reported in the press and on television. The level of shared indignation in the room rises until everyone is talking loudly to everyone else, which is just as well because the notes have fallen to the floor in complete disorder. The chairman tries to bring the meeting to a close, but no one hears him.

Middy corners me for my overdue subscription, £6, and while I look for my chequebook, she asks if I think that allotments may become an important reservoir for unmodified vegetables in the way that they have for old-fashioned varieties which commercial nurseries no longer stock, either because they are less productive than modern versions or because they have fallen foul of bureaucratic regulations. She has an allotment not far from mine and is an organic purist. If I have a problem about whether something I want to do is organically approved I either refer to her for advice, or wait until she is not looking and do it anyway.

'They could be,' I say. 'And that could make allotments important places deserving protection. Which could mean some government funding for us.'

Her partner, Theo, dashes my wishful thinking. 'You heard what the speaker said about pollen sometimes being blown for hundreds of miles. There will be no allotment sites anywhere out of range of pollen drift from G.M. crops.' It is a gloomy note on which to end the evening.

Friday
A council lorry delivers a large cardboard flatpack. This is it. The composter. It was made in Sweden and the instructions baffle me – they are a series of numbered drawings without words. I am still sitting on the hall floor, surrounded by panels, trying to work out what screws on to what and where when my older boy comes in from school. He sizes the situation up immediately and makes a run for the kitchen, but I was expecting this and grab him by the ankle.

'Dad!' he cries in protest.

'It will only take you a minute,' I say, with an ingratiating smile. I stopped feeling humiliated about being shown up for a practical and technological incompetent by my children years ago and learnt to exploit their natural talents. When he was five, the eldest showed me how to set the video and I still haven't got the hang of it. Computer problems which tie me up in knots for an hour are sorted out by one of them with half a dozen keyboard moves executed with the eye-deceiving swiftness of a magician. I never succeed in following the moves and the boys can never explain what they have done in a way I can understand. The questions I ask make them sneer at my ignorance. This must be the generation gap.

We negotiate an adjustment to his pocket money in return for help in setting the composter up on the plot tomorrow.

The Hon. Sec. telephones to ask if I will join the committee of the Allotment Association. I am honoured, but the catch is that committee members have to run the Trading Hut on Saturdays and Sundays – the only time the family can do things together, and not always then. I hum and haw and wriggle out of it, but feel guilty and promise to take him for a drink soon to discuss helping out in other ways.

Saturday

A watery sun gives a hint of warmth as the boy and I deposit the flatpack on the plot. The first thing is to find the right spot for it. The bank of three home-made bins are in the south-eastern corner of the plot, beside the water tank and under the blackthorn which provides sloes for the gin. They are made from builders' pallets and doors rescued from skips, and it might seem that they are more than enough for one allotment. But they are not.

The First Rule of Allotments is: You cannot ever have too much compost.

One of the bins is being filled with fresh stable manure as I get hold of it, though it is so big that I have never yet succeeded in filling it to the top. The second is for maturing stable manure. It is best to let it weather for at least a year, even two, before using it directly around plants, despite what Saleem says. The third is for woody things, cabbage and broccoli stalks, pea and bean vines, the stems of sweetcorn and sunflower, which take forever to break down.

As well as kitchen scraps as the council desires, the new bin will be filled with anything which will rot quickly, like sappy green weeds which have not seeded. Some people add the contents of their vacuum cleaners, but I am not that dedicated. The makers say if it is placed in full sun so the thermoplastic casing can heat up, it will produce usable compost in between six weeks and three months.

There is no room beside the old bins. I don't want it beside the shed in case it smells and attracts flies, but it should be somewhere easily accessible. It can't go on one of the sub-plots because it will get in the way. The same goes for the paths.

'There you are,' says the lad, breaking into my reverie. He has single-handedly assembled the composter just to one side of the cross formed by the meeting of the internal paths. It is square and sturdy with a brooding presence. There is a strange familiarity about it, as if I have seen it many times before in a different setting. Then I get it. If there was a blue lamp on top, and it was bigger, it would be the Tardis, the time-travelling police box from the children's television series *Dr Who*.

I have brought along two plastic bags of vegetable peelings, mouldy bread, leftover pasta and dried mashed potato. I tip these in and they vanish into the depths, then I fasten the lid and listen for the distinctive sound the Tardis makes when it sets off for distant galaxies, a cross between a lion's roar and a grinding waste disposer. There is nothing but birdsong, underscored by what sounds like a duck quacking somewhere. It is only some time later that I realise the council has not sent me the chart to record what goes into the composter.

Sunday

A lovely bright, warm day, and when I push open the gates in the late morning I do a double take. There are so many people about that I wonder if something is on that I have forgotten about, like a start-of-season sale at the Trading Hut. No: they have been brought out by the sun. The rooks and magpies who have had the place largely to themselves all winter must be looking down from the surrounding trees at the throng and remarking sagely to one another: 'Humans on the wing, first sign of spring.' I hope they are right and this is not a false start. Keep reminding myself that February is a treacherous month so that I won't go mad and start planting tomatoes.

I have ransacked the kitchen for things to feed the Tardis and at the back of the fridge found a Christmas pudding, barely nibbled and as dark and dense as coal. This is a major test. If it can digest that, it can digest anything. I notice that Confucius has a wooden compost bin on his allotment which is heaped to the top. On closer inspection it turns out to be full of huge heads of broccoli, untouched loaves of bread and sacks of carrots, all looking perfect. My Inner Saxon Peasant quivers. He is consumed by compost envy and wants it all.

Confucius is very alternative, the last of the hippies, and was given his nickname by his daughter when he grew a wispy beard. Find him on his knees preparing a circular bed for herbs. 'Where did you get this lot?' I ask, a note of accusation creeping into my voice despite myself.

'From the organic greengrocers. I go there twice a week and take everything that is past its sell-by date.'

'You could eat this. It is better than most of the stuff people here grow.'

He smiles. 'I know. Crazy isn't it.'

I had no idea there was an organic greengrocery nearby, but when I ask him about it he becomes vague. I can't blame him. If I had a source of compost material like that, I would keep quiet about it, too. The Tardis is still there, warm to the touch in the sun. The pudding disappears inside and there's a dull thud. If I want compost from it this season, I must find a way of filling it up quickly.

One of my neighbours, Magic, is standing underneath his cherry tree gazing rapturously up. I follow his gaze, looking for a cat or an exotic bird. There is a kestrel about which sometimes perches in Alan's apple tree.

'Man,' he says. 'Look at that abundance, just look at it.' I refocus my eyes and see that the tree is covered in buds with yellowish tips where they are preparing to open. There are hundreds of them. 'Have you seen the bulbs pushing through the ground, have you seen the buds on the fruit bushes?' He sounds like a breathless little boy in a toy shop. 'Spring is coming with a rush that will knock us off our feet.'

Good, or rather, oh dear, I'd better get a move on. A few minutes later I catch sight of Magic using one of those long-handled spades. His movements are smooth and easy. I rush over and demand like a child: 'Can I have a go, please?' It is not quite the same as the spades I saw on television. They had shafts as long as a rake and this one only comes up to my shoulder. The upper half is covered with rubber, which gives a cushioned grip, and the blade is pointed like an arrow head and cupped instead of being squared off.

'I got it because of my back,' he says. 'It's an Irish spade.'

'Yes?' I say, expecting a punchline, but it isn't a joke. He says

they are being sold at a D.I.Y. store for about £20. I dig half a row for him, discovering quickly that the secret is in the leverage of the long handle. The length and thickness of the handle make it quite a bit heavier than a normal spade. As I lift a load of soil I can feel pressure between the shoulder blades, but that is better than having it on the lower back, my weak point. I must have one, but cannot go now because I am taking the family to the Royal Horticultural Society garden at Wisley this afternoon to buy fruit bushes.

Drop into the Trading Hut to get bone meal and fish, blood and bone powder to top dress the fruit bushes which are already in and to mix with the soil when I plant the new ones. The Ace Cultivator and Sailor are on duty, huddled round the portable gas fire in their coats. The sun may be shining but it has done nothing to warm up the Hut, which is dank as only a damp concrete building can be.

Ace measures the fertiliser out of large metal bins on to scales, then bags it. Bought in this way, it is less than half the garden-centre price, and the Hut still makes a profit. The Ace Cultivator took on an allotment for the first time when he retired five years ago and couldn't bear the thought of sitting around the house. He knew nothing whatever about gardening and taught himself from books. He could be seen going around his plot – the one nearest the east gates and originally overgrown with brambles and nettles – with a book in one hand and another under his arm, underlining passages and making notes in the margins.

Some people thought this was very peculiar and scoffed, but they don't scoff now. Ace made it a challenge not only to learn how to garden but to turn that patch of neglected ground into the best allotment on the site. He did it in two years. He treated it like a job, turning up every day at 9 a.m. and staying till 5 p.m., working to detailed plans with single-minded determination. He also taught himself carpentry from books and built wonderful tool lockers, compost bins with folding lids and chamferred edges, and fences with a system of adjustable wires for the fan training of fruit trees. Now he has three allotments, all of them showpieces. Depending on your point of view, he is either an inspiration or a discouraging model of unmatchable perfection. Sometimes both at once.

Sailor lights a cigarette with shaking fingers. 'The tap's still frozen so we can't even make a perishing cup of tea to warm up. It's worse than being on watch in the North Atlantic.' As if to emphasise this, a mournful quacking foghorn sounds outside.

Monday

The D.I.Y. store has a tiny gardening section hidden away behind its timber yard, and there they are, long-handled forks as well as spades. I buy one of each and take them to the plot to try out. They require a slightly different technique from ordinary tools: essentially, to treat the handle as a lever, as I discovered yesterday, using the left hand as the fulcrum halfway down the shaft and the right at the top to counterbalance the load. The important thing is to resist the temptation to slide the hands down the shaft and closer together as it then becomes hard work.

The fork turns out to be more efficient than the spade. The cupped spade will lift a large load but it makes an untidy hole or trench because of its pointed shape, and the cupping makes it hopeless for cutting a straight edge to a bed. Still, they are comfortable to use and I am very pleased with both of them. In ten minutes I have a heap of weeds which half fills the Tardis.

Tuesday
As I am laying the new fruit bushes on the ground to get the spacing right the Ace Cultivator comes along with an armful of raspberry-cane thinnings. Damn! He offered them and I accepted months ago, and I'd clean forgotten about it. I can't say no because he will be offended – he only gives plants to people he thinks will properly appreciate them, so he is conferring an honour upon me. The three bundles of raspberry canes I bought at Wisley on Sunday turned out to contain twice as many plants as I expected, so the space allocated for them is already going to be crowded. Still, Ace's offerings are the superb Autumn Bliss, which Wisley had sold out of, so I accept gratefully and will just have to double them up.

Apart from the raspberries I bought red- and blackcurrants, gooseberries, tayberries, two more thornless blackberries to add to the two I put in last year, and more rhubarb.

This move into fruit has developed a momentum of its own and available space is rapidly running out. The plot will soon be enclosed by hedges of fruit, and I must remember, as I busily erect more frames of posts and wires on which to fan train the peach and two greengages I put in last year, to leave a gap through which I can get in and out.

As a bonus, the frames should support sweet peas, which I was going to give a miss after last year's flop. I tried to grow them as companion plants with climbing French beans to save on poles and netting, but it turned out to be rather a mess. The sweet peas only reached half their normal height and grew into a tangle which the beans had difficulty getting through. I changed my mind as I can't imagine a plot – or a garden – without sweet peas, and sowed some in the autumn, then decided there weren't enough and ordered more last month.

The peach has flowered early, before anything else. Every branch is covered in bright-pink blossom, turning the tree into a beacon of colour which stands out in the drab allotment landscape like a flame. If left alone, it is likely to produce lots of fruit this summer, weather permitting. We are having quite a few sneaky frosts, and every time one is forecast on the evening news I dash down to the plot and wrap the tree in fluffy white fleece and pull a plastic sack over the top. In the dark the tree looms like a ghost, which keeps the vandals away. In the morning I have to unwrap it carefully so the bees can get at the flowers.

Thursday
That foghorn again. And again. I finish treading soil around the newly planted gooseberries and track it down to the Birdman's plot. Danny, his pet duck, is standing beside the sunken bath which serves as a pond and quacking at the top of his voice.

'It's grief,' says the Birdman. 'He is in a terrible state. His stepmother died a few days ago and now he won't eat or swim. He searches everywhere for her and when he can't find her he quacks like this.'

Danny arrived as a duckling four years ago and adopted a hen called Milly as his mother. They were inseparable, except when Danny took a dip in the sunken bath. But Milly was very old and last week she died. The Birdman bought two more ducks, thinking Danny might be lonely, but he ignored them and has gone on quacking.

Friday
Many of the experts who come along to the church hall to give us talks on gardening have turned out to be refreshingly subversive. Whether it is because they feel at home among fellow enthusiasts, or whether it is the relaxing effects of generous quantities of the Hon. Sec.'s fruit wine, they become expansive, giving away trade secrets and even telling us how to bend the rules. This is what the Bee Man does tonight, and I can see a delighted smile spreading across Confucius's face as he talks.

Confucius has wanted to set up hives on his plot for a long time, but he has been thwarted by neighbouring allotmenteers,

Digger's Diary

who are worried about being stung. They stopped him last time by getting the Manager along to quote obscure Allotment Association rules about forbidden livestock.

It's not as if there aren't lots of bees here anyway. The site must provide the best source of nectar for miles around. The Bee Man explains, without any prompting, how to set up secret hives on allotment sites which disapprove of them. The hive is put inside a shed against a wall. The bees come and go through a tiny opening in the shed wall unnoticed by any but the most nosy of neighbours, and the honey can be removed and the hive cleaned out of sight.

Over in the Fox and Ferret afterwards, Confucius can't stop talking about it and keeps trying to buy the Bee Man more drinks. I have a brainwave. I turn to the Hon. Sec. and say, 'A hive in a shed would be a great deterrent against vandals. A notice on the door saying 'Beware Of Bees. Trespassers Will Be Stung' would make most louts think twice about breaking in, don't you think?'

'If they can read,' he replies with world-weary cynicism, before lifting his glass and draining the last drop.

40

March

Saturday
Following Arthur's advice in *Your Garden Week by Week*, I take down a cardboard box of sweet-pea seedlings to plant against the new trellis to give it a bit of cover and colour while the fruit trees develop. At the moment the greengages, which were planted as maidens, that is, one-year-old trees, last spring are still small and though the three-year-old peach is much bigger it will probably be next year before they all begin to take shape. That is if I get the fan training right, which I am rather nervous about, though the Ace Cultivator says there is nothing simpler. With luck, they should all bear fruit this summer.

41

The Birdman is on the path behind his shed as I pass and he peers into the box and asks: 'What are those?'

'Sweet peas.'

'Sweet peas? They're a sorry-looking bunch.' He's right: they are. These are the ones I sowed in trays in the autumn hoping to produce sturdy plants which would have a head start once spring came. They outgrew the trays after Christmas and became spindly on windowsills indoors, so I transplanted them into pots and put them outside. The move has not done them any good. In fact, they have stopped growing.

I have loved sweet peas ever since I watched my grandfather tending them in his Cumbrian garden when I was five or six. He was usually a craggy and forbidding man who said little, but among his flowers he changed into a gentle and kindly person, and I knew, as children do, that there must be something magical about them to have such an effect.

Sweet peas are one of the few flowers I grow on the allotment, for their delicacy and incomparable scent. A vase of them will fill a room with perfume. They are also next to impossible to buy from a flower shop because once cut they last for only a few days.

The Birdman shakes his head. 'Never transplant sweet peas. They hate having their roots disturbed. Come here and look at these.' He leads me on to his plot, past the big greenhouse full to the roof with seedlings, to the small lean-to greenhouse at the end of his shed. This has a protective covering of netting over a wooden frame to stop vandals from smashing the glass with stones thrown from the lane on the other side of the boundary fence. 'There,' he says with some pride. There are half a dozen very deep florist's pots on a shelf, each full of staked sweet peas nearly 2 feet tall with thick, almost square stems. They make my specimens look sickly. Outside, Danny quacks mournfully. I know how he feels.

'If you can't get these deep pots, you should get hold of some half-litre plastic drink bottles, cut the bottoms off, upend 'em, take the caps off for drainage, and grow sweet peas in those.'

'A greenhouse helps,' I say defensively.

'Do you want one?'

'Well . . .' Yes, I do. But new ones are expensive, and though a greenhouse would help me to start salad crops early and grow a few exotic plants which won't survive outdoors, I have never felt that that alone would justify the cost. There is also the risk that vandals will smash the glass. However, the Birdman is almost certainly talking about one that is second-hand or salvaged, so cagily I ask: 'How much?'

'Leave it with me,' he says with a wink. As I walk on I notice that this end of the site is beginning to pick up. It has quite a few derelict plots, but here and there are signs of regeneration. A home-made shed has gone up on one plot which looks like a Greek temple. The side facing the path is made from pieces of theatrical scenery with four athletic goddesses bearing a painted roof on their heads. That belongs to the Artist and her husband, who arrived last autumn. A shed on an adjoining plot looks like a ranchhouse with a terrace, and inside there is a fitted kitchen with sink, cooker and fridge.

The day has turned cold and overcast and rain threatens. Before it comes I hurriedly plant the sweet peas along the trellis, even though I now doubt whether they will prosper. If they don't, I have more coming on in seed trays at home.

Sunday

I have been forcing one of the rhubarb crowns since December by covering it with a tall chimney pot, found in a skip, with a wooden board over the top to exclude light. The pale-red stalks are now about 18 inches long and slender with a tuft of yellow-green leaves on top. The time has come to pull them.

At home they are chopped into 2-inch lengths and put with sugar into a pan on a low heat until the juice runs. Eaten with nothing added, the taste is wonderful, more delicate and lighter than unforced rhubarb and with none of its coarseness of texture. I can understand why smart restaurants charge the earth for it. Unfortunately, forcing debilitates rhubarb crowns and can permanently damage them, so I only do it with one of my eight plants each year, then rest it the next year.

Digger's Diary

Rhubarb Crumble

Peel, core and slice two Bramley apples and chop 2 pounds of rhubarb into short lengths, simmer in a saucepan with a tablespoon of water, a pinch each of cinnamon and cloves, and sugar to taste for ten minutes. Transfer to pie dish, cover with crumble mix made from 8 oz flour, 5 oz brown sugar, 3 oz butter and baking powder mixed into crumbs and bake for about half an hour.

Crumble can also be used for any other fruits and it is especially good using gooseberries and blackcurrants. A sprinkle of brown sugar on the hot crust makes it irresistible to children. Serve with ice cream, cream or custard.

Monday

Succeed in filling the Tardis to the top after collecting kitchen waste from neighbours and my mother-in-law. Roll up the two carpets on the future potato patch. Under one there is bare earth where all the annual weeds have vanished, though here and there are clumps of yellowish-white tendrils where bindweed and docks amazingly still survive after six months without light. I will have to dig them out.

The other carpet was laid over a thick layer of stable straw, which I hoped would rot down quickly as a result. Only partly successful. What hasn't rotted away has compressed and darkened so that it resembles a well-used coconut mat, and I am about to discover that it hides a horticultural horror.

I start work in a corner with a fork, thinking that once turned in this mat of compost will break down quickly and provide a good bed of nutrients and moisture for the growing potatoes. The fork snags on something instead of coming out cleanly. I pull hard and up it comes, dragging white strings from the ground which go off in all directions. Loose compost falls away leaving the fork holding what looks like a thick bundle of tangled wool. I recognise the fibrous roots of couch grass, one of the gardener's worst enemies, but I have never seen such a dense ball of them.

44

Have I unluckily hit on an isolated outbreak, or is there more? I take two steps to the left and drive the fork into the ground – it snags again on roots. Two steps to the right and the same thing happens. I sink to my knees, appalled, scrabbling with gloved hands among the compost and lifting up skeins of the stuff. I have inadvertently provided ideal conditions for the rapid spread of this awful weed and it has taken full advantage of me.

What to do? My Inner Saxon Peasant wants to borrow a pig to plough the ground with its snout and eat the roots, and then eat the pig himself. Unfortunately, there are no pigs around here to be borrowed, and if there were, I can imagine the consternation it would cause among my fellow allotmenteers.

It takes me a few minutes to calm down, and when I do and investigate further, I realise that I have actually got off fairly lightly and there is no need for such a drastic remedy. The couch grass, invading from paths and a neighbouring plot, has come up into the straw instead of burrowing through the soil. I can bend down and pull it up in handfuls, shake the compost off and load it into the wheelbarrow.

After a while I realise that 'getting off fairly lightly' is a relative term. It's still hard work lifting all those roots. I take a barrowload down to the rubbish skip near the Trading Hut and encounter Ali, who has a plot adjoining the railway line. He is a fellow back sufferer and has ingeniously adapted his wheelbarrow to do away with bending and lifting. He has attached a pair of pram wheels to the back legs and bent the handles upright so that the barrow can be pushed like a cart.

'My friend,' he says, 'why be a donkey when you can be a camel?' I take this to be an Arab proverb and nod wisely, though I have no idea what it means.

Tuesday
Poppy stops me as I trundle past her plot with another load of couch-grass roots for the skip. 'Don't throw it away,' she chides like a careful housewife. 'Compost it.'

'This stuff?' I ask incredulously, and stir the roots with a fork to make sure she sees it for what it is. She nods. 'But it has just survived six months under a carpet, and any that goes into the compost bin accidentally takes root and grows like fury. It can't be composted.' I usually burn it, but there is a council clamp-down on bonfires after complaints from nearby householders that smoke is ruining washing hanging out on lines. In a few weeks everyone will be having bonfires again, but for now we are being good.

'It can, but not in the usual way. It has to be excluded from all light and water for a year which means putting it into black plastic sacks. Then you get this . . .' She fetches a greengrocer's wooden box which has been lined with polythene and filled with humus, picks up a handful and lets it trickle through her fingers. It is fine and dark and rich looking. 'It makes the best compost for raising seeds. I am just about to plant this with parsley.'

I am impressed. But more than that, turning a pernicious weed into seed compost appeals to my sense of poetic justice. Yesss! That'll teach it.

I turn the barrow around, dump the roots on to a rolled-up carpet and hurry off to the builders' merchants for heavy-duty rubble sacks. I have used ordinary dustbin sacks around the plot before to collect weeds and they are useless because they tear as soon as you look at them. By the end of the afternoon, six bulging sacks are lined up beside the path on the Ridgeway, their necks fastened with twisted wire, and I feel great satisfac-tion. And exhaustion.

Lift the lid on the Tardis before leaving to see how the com-posting is coming on. Slowly. Wonder why the slices of bread have developed scalloped edges.

Wednesday
I find that I am listening for something which isn't there and it takes me time to work out that it is Danny. I haven't heard him quack all morning. On the way home for lunch I stop at the

Birdman's, fearing that he may have died from grief. But Danny is there, surrounded by half a dozen plump red hens scratching the ground, and even I can tell that he is one very blissful duck. All the hens look exactly like Milly.

'That's clever of you,' I say to the Birdman.

'Desperation,' he replies. 'I couldn't stand that quacking any more, and when I threatened to eat him, the missus threatened to boil my head.'

That was a happy ending, except for the Birdman. He had hoped to give up poultry keeping when Milly died so that he would not have to come down first thing every day to open the hen house. 'I was really looking forward to having a lie-in at weekends,' he sighs.

Friday

Add more loaves, pasta and chips to the Tardis. The slices of bread with scalloped edges have developed holes like Swiss cheese, so something is going on. They have also turned blue and furry and there are black specks everywhere.

There are a lot of worms in the soil where the carpets were, especially the area covered by manure. They are sleek and fat, and if they have done their job properly of carrying digested manure down into the ground, that is how my potatoes should look in midsummer. Worms give an accurate indication of the health of the soil. When I first took the allotment, I knew the ground was exhausted because it was grey and there was hardly a worm to be found on it. Those that did appear were as thin as bootlaces and almost inert. Worms live off decaying vegetable matter in the soil, and mine were starving because there was so little of it.

Alan, who took me under his wing the day I arrived to look for a suitable allotment and directed me towards this one, did warn me that the soil needed building up and putting in good heart. He said the previous occupant had cropped nothing but potatoes off it for many years. They take a lot out of the ground and he had never put anything back except some chemicals, and worms cannot live off those. But the allotment was worth taking, Alan said, because the soil was basically sound and easy to work and it was in a good position with an attractive square shape. All it needed was plenty of muck. It's had that all right. I reckon I dug about 5 tons of stable manure into it in the first few years before I noticed any real improvement, and I keep putting on as much more of it as I can get hold of. Now, the soil is dark and every spadeful has several wriggly tenants. Cow manure is even better, but there are no dairy farms nearby.

The birds have been at the onion sets again. About a dozen have been pulled out of the ground and thrown aside. Do the birds think the tops peeping out of the soil are worms, or are they looking for nesting material? I crawl uncomfortably along on hands and knees between the rows to replant them while trying to avoid squashing any. The sets haven't had time to form proper roots, so they are not damaged, though they probably will be now as, ignoring Saleem's advice, I shove them straight back into the ground without making new holes.

The sixth sense again, that prickling on the nape of the neck, warns me that I am being watched. I look over my shoulder and my blood runs cold.

A figure in a combat jacket, face hidden by a gas mask, is standing on the path on the far side of the allotment pointing a weapon with a long, narrow barrel at me. Has war been declared? Who with? Is he a paratrooper, a saboteur? And why is my allotment a military target?

These crazy questions and even more crazy answers race through my mind as I try to scramble to my feet. It is difficult because my legs have gone wobbly, but I refuse to die on my knees in the mud.

As I get up the soldier advances across the plot jerking the weapon at me, and I raise my hands. The mask is what really frightens me. A bullet offers a quick, clean death, but a squirt of nerve or mustard gas would be agonising.

'Whur?' The sound through the mask is barely intelligible. What language is it?

I swallow nervously and ask: 'What?' The weapon points at the ground and makes a circular then a stabbing motion.

'Hur ur thur?'

'Sorry. I don't know what you mean.' As I speak I am mentally measuring the distance to the shed and wondering if I can run behind it before he has time to shoot. The weapon is jerked up and a babble of strange words pours out as if I have made him angry. 'Sorry,' I repeat, like the craven coward I am. 'Just don't shoot.' The words stop, then start again, only this time they run together like laughter.

The hand not holding the weapon pulls the gas mask down to reveal Chicken Tom, laughing his head off.

'What are you doing?' I demand, failing to see anything funny. 'You frightened the life out of me.'

' "Don't shoot",' he says, and doubles up with laughter. I cross my arms and adopt a pose of wounded dignity and a severe expression.

Chicken Tom has come by on a long-standing arrangement to test the acid level of my soil. The 'weapon' is a pH meter with a long metal probe on a pistol grip for pushing into the ground. He is wearing a gas mask – goodness knows where he got it from – because he recently became ill after shifting a load of stable manure on to his plot. He thinks the manure was giving off fumes from some noxious chemicals used to treat either the straw or the horses and he is taking no chances.

His symptoms were palpitations, sweating, insomnia and a feeling of having a head full of gas. I glance across at the stable manure that I am digging in on the potato patch. It looks harmless enough, but nowadays, who can be sure? Am I feeling sweaty, gassy, sleepless? Well, now I think about it . . .

'What about seeing a doctor?'

His hands fly up like startled pigeons. 'I've seen three, my G.P. and two at the hospital. They've tested my heart and my blood and my kidneys and my this and my that, and what do they do?' I shake my head encouragingly. 'Give me pills for anxiety. Anxiety,' he repeated with disgust. 'I told them they should be down here testing the manure. That's where the trouble is.'

Mindful of the manure a few feet away, I offer to leave it to another day, but he nobly insists on keeping his promise, though he puts the gas mask back in place before starting. The soil turns out to be mildly acidic with a pH of about 5.

He stands up and removes the gas mask so he can speak. 'When I tested mine, the pointer went completely off the dial on the acid side. That was because I had been putting fresh manure from my chicken run on it for years. I'd often wondered why I couldn't grow cabbages. Still, it was easy to put right with a few bags of lime. You won't need much here. Only remember not to put any where the potatoes are going in or they'll go all scabby.'

Tuesday
Traditionally, potatoes are planted on Good Friday; I don't know why. This year Easter is late, and as I have finished digging over the potato bed, I decide not to wait. The seed potatoes, the 3 kilos of Charlotte second earlies I ordered from the Hut and 2 kilos of Pink Fir Apple I bought on impulse from a garden centre, have been chitting in egg boxes on the sill of a north-facing bedroom window. Chitting means encouraging the seeds

to sprout. Chitted potatoes start to grow more quickly than unchitted ones, which means an earlier crop. The sprouts should be about an inch long and care must be taken not to knock these off when they are planted. I get out the orange marker line and excavate shallow trenches with the draw hoe, put the potatoes in and draw a slight ridge of earth up over them. If I wasn't organic, I would have sprinkled Growmore fertiliser in the trenches. The organic alternative is a layer of comfrey leaves under the potatoes. My comfrey is late this year and I fear that if I strip the baby leaves off now, the plants will suffer later in the season. The rotted stable manure should make up for it.

I don't grow main-crop potatoes because they take up too much land. Pink Fir Apples are a main-crop variety but I treat them like an early and will lift from July onwards for use as a salad potato.

Saturday
Spring arrives quite suddenly – the real thing, not the false promise of a few weeks ago. I always thought it crept in bit by bit over several weeks, but this year it comes, 'pop', just like that. I turn up at the plot muffled against a bitter and prolonged north wind in layers of clothing which make me look like the Michelin man. As I work the wind moves softly round to the south-west, the clouds part to let the sun through and the temperature starts to climb, though I am so engrossed in what I am doing that I don't notice at first.

The coat and cap come off, then the bodywarmer and scarf, and finally the sweater and waistcoat – well, it has been very cold. When I pause to roll up my shirtsleeves, I suddenly realise that the quality of sunlight has changed. It has lost the thin, anaemic wateriness of winter and has become rich and golden, the sort of light which makes plants grow in front of your eyes. And then I do notice things: the brilliant green of the garlic spears rising out of the ground, the glorious daffodils, the buds almost visibly swelling, and the early fruit blossom in delicate pinks and whites.

It is extraordinary, as if I have just removed a pair of dark glasses. The air is clean and fresh and invigorating. I understand the euphoria that country people must always have felt when they realised, like me, that winter was over. It is too good a moment to waste on digging. I throw the spade down, seized by an irresistible urge to sing and dance. I do a little hop and a skip, a sort of soft-shoe shuffle in the cabbage patch, then stop guiltily to see if anyone is looking at me askance. No, but I decide instead to go for a walk in the sunshine. Everyone I meet is cheerful, smiling and happy.

The Ace Cultivator is on his knees in front of one of his plum trees, carefully rubbing out buds which are facing the wrong way. He has fan trained these, and the peaches, beautifully and the sight of them in fruit in high summer inspired me to try the same. But now my trees are in I hesitate to touch them in case I make a mess of it, and wish that I had bought ready-trained ones, though they are much more expensive.

'There is nothing simpler,' he repeats when I again confess my fear of making a mess of the pruning. 'These all began as one-year-old basic bush varieties and I taught myself how to shape them by trial and error.'

'My trials will lead to a lot of errors,' I say.

'No, no. You're being too pessimistic. What you do is this.' He selects a branch and ties it to a bamboo cane that is itself tied at an angle of about 45 degrees across horizontal wires. 'This is called a rib. Cut it back by half to an upward-facing bud, here. The shoot from that should be tied in as it grows. Any shoots growing the wrong way must be rubbed out, like this, and this. All right?' He sits back on his heels and looks at me. I nod hesitantly.

'If you make mistakes, it usually won't matter. Fruit trees are vigorous things, putting out far more growth than you want. If you prune in the wrong place, the tree will grow around it in such a way that you will be able to correct the mistake in time.' I nod again. I'm sure he is right, but pruning is one of my blind spots, like not being able to draw a straight line or hang wallpaper or, long ago, learn my mathematical tables. The more I try, the worse I become. It is irrational and childish, and I refuse to give in to it, especially with the exuberance of spring all around.

'Do you want me to show you one more time?' Ace sounds like Miss White, the kindly maths teacher who took me endlessly through tables at primary school without ever suggesting that I was being stupid for not remembering them.

'Please.'

He takes another branch and repeats the process and looks at me with an expectant smile, and offers to come over and show me where to start on mine. 'O.K., but I think I understand now.' I don't know that I do, but if I don't, I am not going to let it spoil the first day of spring, so I leap up and set off again on my tour of inspection. Poppy emerges from her shed, which is painted a smoky blue to coordinate with the bottles and forget-me-nots, and waves to me. She is wearing black leggings and a black T-shirt, and in one hand is a bottle of wine and in the other three glasses.

'Carlo, come and join us,' she calls to her husband, who is out of sight. She puts the glasses on the table in the arbour and pours. 'Can you feel it?' she asks, and wriggles with pleasure.

'Spring?'

'Yes. Isn't it wonderful?' Carlo emerges from the undergrowth like a latter-day explorer, wearing shorts and a beach hat and carrying a pair of shears.

'How did you know it was going to be so warm today?' I ask.

'Ah,' says Poppy, and smiles mysteriously. Perhaps the plants told her. The wine is a Chilean cabernet sauvignon, which Poppy says she drinks for its health-giving properties, so I expect it to taste like cough medicine, but it is excellent. I smack my lips over the last drops, regretfully refuse a second glass, and head off, smiling and waving to everyone and being smiled and waved at as if we are all taking part in a toothpaste commercial. Everyone but the Birdman. I can't see him anywhere.

It is such a day of universal goodwill that I ignore the allotment etiquette which says you never walk on to someone else's plot unless invited, and walk down the path beside the greenhouse, waving through the open shed door to Molly who is feeding the rabbits. There is a sheltered spot at the bottom, behind the hen house, and the Birdman is stooping over a double row of drainpipes. They are sticking out of the ground close together, the tallest on the outside and the shortest in the middle, as if he has buried a church organ.

'What have you got here?' He jumps as if I've poked him with a thorny stick.

'Oh, it's you,' he says with relief. 'There's no one else with you is there?' I shake my head. 'Not Five Pints?'

He is the Birdman's deadliest rival in the annual allotment show in the autumn. They fight it out each year for the highest marks and the Best Exhibitor award – a sort of allotment Top Gun. He checks behind me to make sure I am telling the truth.

'What is it?' I ask, my curiosity thoroughly aroused.

'Parsnips,' he hisses in a stage whisper. 'And carrots.' He leads me back to the pipes. They are filled nearly to the top with a gritty mixture of sand and soil from which a few leaves show. 'It's my secret weapon for the autumn show. Growing them in these means they will grow straight and long, like pipes themselves. The mixture is important: sandy with low fertility; in fact, for carrots, the poorer the soil the better. Then down they go looking for food.'

I am impressed. He is already preparing for the show more than six months beforehand, and I have not yet sorted out my sowing programme for next week. I say, 'My carrots always grow into twisted, corkscrew shapes. They taste all right but they look weird.'

'That's either because you've got stony soil . . .' I shake my head. 'Or there's too much manure in it.' I nod. 'You've got to keep carrots hungry to keep them on the straight and narrow.' He laughs, then becomes serious. 'Don't tell anyone what I said, will you?' I promise. 'My secret weapon must stay secret.'

Tuesday
The peas are growing fast and need support. I keep a roll of chicken wire in the tool locker for this purpose. I unroll it and set

it up in a double row, held upright by a dozen bamboo canes threaded through the wire. Many of the lower leaves have holes in the edges. Could be birds eating them or pea weevils. Hope it's not the latter as they infest the peas with maggots. Horrible things.

In case it is birds, I set up several spinning-bottle scarers. This is a very ingenious and simple technique I am copying from other allotmenteers. Fetch half a dozen empty 2-litre plastic bottles from the shed and cut five vertical flaps in the sides. These are bent out at right angles to the bottle. Cut a hole in the bottom and slip over a 2- to 3-foot bamboo cane set upright beside the peas and beans. The slightest breeze catches the flaps like sails and set the bottles spinning. Birds are frightened by the movement and will not settle to feed anywhere near them.

The broad beans are flowering already though they are barely half-grown. Inspect them closely for slug damage. They seem all right in that respect, although they are a bit droopy. The ground is dry and as it has not rained for some time, a few weeks now that I think of it, I get the watering can and give beans and peas a good soaking. The tank is getting low because the main supply has not been switched on yet after the winter shut-down to prevent frost bursting the pipes.

As I am standing in front of the peach trying to visualise it in years to come, pruned and unpruned, Saleem's wife, Rita, and the Artist join me to admire it. I explain my dilemma. I ordered a one-year-old tree so that it would be easy to train. Instead of a Maiden, the nursery sent me a three-year-old (a Matron, perhaps?), which was all they had. They probably thought they were giving me a bargain, as they did not charge extra for it. It has grown rapidly in the past year, developing a sturdy trunk about 5 feet high to a point where it divides naturally into three strong branches. These are already reaching beyond the top of the 8-foot-high trellis. Below the main branches the trunk carries a dozen or so much smaller, twiggy branches.

'I have to cut it off down there,' I say, indicating a place about 18 inches above the ground and just above a pair of the puny twigs.

They are both horrified. Ace joins us and I ask him if such a radical pruning might kill the tree.

'Maybe,' he says. 'It's a pity you didn't start with something smaller. But it is the only way if you want a fan.'

Rita and the Artist turn on him, accusing him of wanting to mutilate a fine tree. Rita, who is growing a peach as an espalier with just two pairs of branches growing out along horizontal wires, says I should leave mine as it is and train the top three branches into a fan.

The Artist says she wants to paint it. 'It is so pretty. I can't bear the thought of it being cut down to a stump in the ground.'

Ace smiles in sympathy but is unmoved by the protests. He says to me: 'If you don't prune it back severely, all the lower branches will gradually die off, leaving you with a bare trunk topped by three big branches which you won't be able to train because they will be growing way above the trellis where the fruit will be out of reach.'

Oh, dear. What to do? While I think about it, go and dig up and shift a thornless blackberry growing against the wall of the shed. It has already outgrown the site, despite putting out just one new cane in the year since it was planted.

But what a cane. It is more than 20 feet long. Find a gap on the trellis between a greengage and a tayberry and, as space is limited, train the cane up and down the frame in a series of tight loops. All the time as I work my glance is being drawn to the peach.

At home I look up every reference to fan training in my gardening books, and they all side with the Ace Cultivator.

Thursday
I am bending over the blackcurrant bushes trying to dust the soil with bone meal without getting it on the young leaflets when Sailor hails me from the path. I know I should have done this job in January but I forgot, and expect that is what he is going to tell me. Instead, he confounds me with the word: 'Foxes.'

'Foxes? Where?' I ask, looking around.

He nods meaningfully at the bag in my gloved hand and somehow manages to shake his head discouragingly at the same time. I look at the bag with misgiving. I always handle bone meal reluctantly and with care because of the remote possibility that it may be infected with B.S.E. or some other animal disease, but it is the best source of slow-release nitrogen and phosphate available to the organic gardener, so I need to use it. Is there some new outrage involving food products that I haven't heard about?

'Here. You'll have them all over the place.' He lights a cigarette and coughs. 'They smell the meal and think it must be proper bones and go frantic. They'll dig up those bushes looking for them if you're not careful.'

'Oh, no. What can I do to stop them?'

'Nothing,' he says, and walks off with a cheerful smile, not realising the anxiety he has caused me. He stops briefly and calls back: 'You could try mothballs, or rags soaked in creosote. It confuses their sense of smell.'

Ah. I know people who put mothballs in among their pea seeds to deter mice from eating them, so it might work.

Friday
A countryside ranger from the local council has come along to the church hall tonight to enlist our help in protecting wildlife. He wants us to leave untidy corners on our plots, piles of prunings and old lumber if possible, where creatures can hide, and to let some weeds, like nettles, flourish.

He says, 'An old lady I know left a heap of raspberry prunings in her garden for several months, and when she asked me to move it for her, I found a hundred froglets sheltering under them. And as you know, frogs eat all sorts of garden pests.'

In his terms I am running a model wildlife allotment, which makes me feel better about my untidiness. He also makes a strong plea for everyone to adopt organic methods, which will benefit all wild creatures.

This is timely, as the Orgies have launched a recruitment drive. Of the 140 plots on our site, only about half a dozen of the tenants are also Orgies, though I am sure many more cultivate organically. So it should be fertile ground for new members.

The ranger answers a question which has long puzzled me. Why are there no hedgehogs rootling around allotments, which should be the ideal environment for them? I have never seen one, yet I would dearly like to have some to keep the slugs down.

And there's the rub.

Hedgehogs eat slugs which have been poisoned with slug pellets and die themselves. It turns out that the top-selling product in the Trading Hut last year was metaldehyde, the toxic chemical used in slug pellets and other pest killers. Maybe we could turn this into a rallying cry for the Orgies – Save A Hedgehog: Go Organic.

I remember when every Citroen 2CV and Morris Minor had a Save The Whale bumper sticker. We could do the same for hedgehogs.

Sunday

The clocks moved on to summer time last night and the extra hour of daylight in the evening has changed the whole tempo of the allotments. Somehow it seems to make far more time available than just an extra hour on the clock. The odd thing is that I feel I can get more done by taking things more slowly, like a car moving from second to fourth gear and travelling faster, even though the engine is turning slower. Working in the evening as the light slowly fades has a more soothing rhythm to it than daytime working.

Or perhaps it is just that I know the days are going to get longer, warmer, and sunnier until the whole summer lies before me, and I love it. It has even touched Mad Alice. She has woven a circle of spring flowers around the brim of her hat.

April

Wednesday

I pass through the gates into a strange and barely recognisable world. Everywhere the landscape is filled with clouds of delicate white and pink blossom, more shades of pink than a paint-maker's catalogue. It does what the snow did in February: miraculously transforms the allotments into a place of beauty. The fruit trees, the blackthorn, hawthorn and lilac have flowered together and in voluptuous profusion. Does this indicate a long, hot summer to come?

It uplifts everyone. They raise their heads from the job in hand and look at the flowers and smile, and remark to each other how lovely the blossom is this spring. But only for a moment, because there is too much to do, and at the back of everyone's mind is the nagging worry about the shortage of water. It has hardly rained for the past six weeks and the ground is already caked and cracking in many places.

I make a long detour to admire the blossom and see what people are doing at the west end of the site. This is where many of the old-timers have their plots and some of them are show-pieces. I am in unfamiliar territory, and it is only when I hear a saxophone playing that I realise that I must be close to Five Pints's allotment. His wife won't let him play at home, so he comes down here to practise, fuelled by several bottles of cider, and as the cider goes down the saxophone becomes more wistful and sad. His plot is immaculate.

Friday
Everything is growing so fast that I can almost feel the allotment throb with energy as it soaks up the sun. Wherever I look, Mother Nature is romping away into the green distance and I am floundering along in her wake unable to keep up.

Today is one of those days when I seem to wake up half an hour behind the rest of the world and no matter how hard I run, I never catch up. Perhaps others feel the same. Everyone on the site is hard at work, backs bent and heads down with no time for an idle gossip or even a greeting. Time and tide *and* spring wait for no man. Suddenly, a hundred jobs need to be done at once, more if I include the maintenance chores I should have done over the winter instead of sitting snugly by the fire with a pile of gardening catalogues. Well, that's my own fault, and the loose hinges on the shed door, the leak in the roof, the collapsing fence and the rest will just have to wait a bit longer.

After two hours of rushing around the plot forking, pruning, planting, composting and tying-in, the work still to be done seems to have increased, as if new jobs have sprung up like dragon's teeth behind my back. Yet, at the end of the day when I step back on to the Ridgeway for an overview, the plot does look good: fertile, productive and not too disorderly, despite weeds erupting, especially among the onions.

When I put the tools away, a pamphlet falls off a shelf where I put it unread after idly picking it up in the Hut. It is titled 'Why Have An Allotment?' and on the front page it says just an hour's work each weekend in the winter will get a small plot into shape for spring planting. Ha!

When I lift the lid on the Tardis, I see that the level has fallen slightly which I take to be a sign that the mysterious process of composting is working well. Also notice a circular hole in one corner with black specks around it. Could I have a mouse?

Asparagus shoots are breaking the surface, four or five of them, as thick as the handle on my trowel. They should be ready within a week. Before going home I pick over the purple-sprouting broccoli, probably for the last time. The half-dozen plants have cropped well for nearly four months. I shall let the rest of the curds flower for the bees and set seed for the birds. The small heads on long, slender stalks are so unlike the hefty supermarket broccoli, which could be mistaken for green cauliflowers, that they could be completely different plants. The purple-sprouting broccoli has the admirable habit of producing more curds the more it is cut. The curds need careful cooking. Unlike the supermarket broccoli, they go limp and soggy if boiled a fraction too long, so the best way is to steam them for just a couple of minutes and serve them slightly crisp.

According to Arthur I should be preparing celery trenches, training cucumbers, sowing cauliflowers, globe artichokes, kohl rabi, salsify and . . . the list is endless. He was really ahead of his time in 1936 in growing vegetables which are still considered exotic today. I did not encounter a globe artichoke until I was in my early twenties and had no idea how to eat it when it was put in front of me.

A dozen pigeons are circling the steeple of St Jude's, etched against the pink and aquamarine sky where the sun is setting. That usually means the weather is about to change.

Monday

This is it: the day that I must tackle the new fruit trees. If I put off pruning them any longer it will be too late. The wood will grow too big and stiff to bend into a fan shape without splitting. At the root of my procrastination is the fear that I will damage the trees by cutting off branches when they are growing vigorously early in the season. It goes back to the time I pruned a grape vine in the spring and it virtually bled to death as the sap poured from wounds which refused to heal.

I keep telling myself that stone fruit are different and must be pruned when the sap is running because this helps prevent disease from infecting the cut wood. My father once trimmed a Victoria plum in the dormant season at the same time that he was cutting back apple trees, and it developed canker and died. It was a splendid, broad canopied tree in its prime, and he was so upset that he wouldn't so much as take a twig off a plum after that. That experience reinforced my impression that fruit trees are difficult and temperamental to deal with and best left to experts.

'Courage,' I mutter to myself as I kneel in front of the peach with the booklet on growing fruit produced by Ken Muir, the nurseryman from whom I bought the trees. I put the open booklet on the ground and compare the tree with the illustrations. I tell myself sternly that if the Ace Cultivator did it this way, so can I. If the worst comes to the worst, I can always get a new tree and start again.

Pick up the tree loppers and, with a muttered apology to the tree, cut the stem with a sharp jerk. The top falls to the ground. Open a tin of Arbrex and paint the wound to stop it becoming diseased, then tie two bamboo canes on to the trellis at an angle rather less than 45 degrees and tie the side branches on to these. They look uneven because they don't quite match and one has an uncomfortable kink where it wants to come forward. These will become the ribs from which shoots will produce the fan of new branches. Once that happens I will remove the twiggy branches lower down the main stem and rub out any buds pointing in the wrong direction before they break.

I sit back on my heels and brush the sweat off my forehead. It may not look as neat as the tree in the illustrations, but it will do for a beginning. Now for the greengages. They are smaller and I snip, snip the first into shape in a minute, but the second gives me pause. It has three good lateral branches, two which tie against the trellis and a third midway between them which curves out in a graceful arch over the plot. Is it possible to have a hybrid between a fan and a bush? I look at it from different angles and try to imagine it fully grown. It would be a strange, lop-sided thing if grown like that in the open, and with the weight all on one side it would blow down in the first westerly gale, but against the trellis it might work very well.

'Would you be happy with that shape?' I ask, thinking aloud.

'Talking to yourself?' says the Birdman from the other side of the trellis. 'First sign of madness. Do you know what the second one is?'

'No.'

'Well, it's . . .'

'I mean, I wasn't talking to myself.'

'Oh. Talking to the plants, eh?' His face, framed by one of the small squares of the trellis, takes on a pitying expression. 'I suppose that's not so bad. Unless the plants start answering back,' and he breaks into a raucous laugh which sends the rooks flapping up from Magic's cabbage seedlings. I do occasionally offer my plants a word of encouragement or praise, but I don't talk to them properly because I would be embarrassed to be caught at it like this. But many people do, and there is research which claims to have proved that plants grow better when they are talked to. Poppy goes further and plays the radio to her plants. Mostly light classical music, though she reckons they really love listening to the daily instalments of those country folk, *The Archers*, on Radio Four. When the theme tune comes on, an unnatural stillness falls on the plot as the plants settle down to fifteen minutes of drama and pathos.

'Have you got a minute?' says the Birdman. 'I've got that greenhouse you were asking for.' I was? 'It's really cheap. Just thirty pounds.' No matter. This sounds good. 'There it is,' he says when we reach his plot. He indicates a jumble of glass panes and plastic sheets, some painted white, leaning against the hen house. Beside them are aluminium struts, many of them bent, and a fertiliser sack of nuts and bolts. My heart sinks. But it was unrealistic to expect a new greenhouse in neat flatpacks for £30, and that is still a good price for a second-hand one. 'It's all there,' he says. 'I took it down myself from a fellow over by the Common who wanted the space.'

'Have you got the instructions for putting it up?' I ask.

'Instructions?' He sounds offended, as if the word is mildly blasphemous. 'You don't need instructions. Just take one bit of metal and bolt it on to another. You had a Meccano set as a lad, didn't you?' I nod unhappily. I could never make anything with it apart from a catapult, and that kept falling apart. 'Well, there you are then. Oh, and talking about space, could you shift it in the next day or two? I've got something else coming in.' He twinkles at me.

The Birdman is a regular visitor to markets and car-boot sales, and all sorts of things make a brief appearance beside his shed, to be done up and then passed on – mowers, mechanical cultivators and bird cages. He has such a natural flair for fixing things that he must have been born with a screwdriver in his hand, and this makes it difficult for him to understand that other people may not be as handy.

There is a scream from the other side of the fence to my left. Rita has one hand over her mouth and is staring at the peach.

'Oh, no,' she says. 'I never thought you would do it.'

Wednesday
Transplant the French beans into small pots at home because they have outgrown the seed trays and are getting leggy in the competition for light. The runner beans are threatening to go the same way. The pots and trays are laid out on a concrete path

against the south-facing wall of the kitchen. It is a warm and sheltered spot which encourages growth.

Go down to the plot after lunch and wave to the Artist. She pointedly turns her back, not speaking to me. Rita must have told her about the pruning. They will forgive me if the peach tree survives, but will it?

Erect supports for the beans, using 8-foot bamboo poles for the runners and cheaper 6-foot ones for the climbing French beans, which don't grow as tall. Notice again that quite a few people still follow the traditional technique of digging double trenches for beans in the autumn which are gradually filled up with the stems and leaves of brassicas and vegetable peelings. The main drawback with this system is apparent wherever I look – the stems and peelings have not rotted down, at least not on the surface, because they cannot generate any heat in the shallow and uncovered trenches. They will not yield much in the way of nutrients to the growing beans, though they may break down faster when the trenches are covered with earth. The process of decomposition also takes nitrogen out of the soil which will make the growing beans unhappy, but at least all those leaves and peelings will hold plenty of moisture, which is essential for all beans.

I mark out lines for the first pair of trenches, about 2 feet apart, and excavate them a full spade deep. Barrowloads of rotted manure from the compost bins go into the trenches and the soil is put back in a saucer shape so that there is a depression running the length of the trenches to hold water. The poles go into the ground in pairs, just beyond the outer lips of the depression. I start with a pair at each end, leaning slightly inwards so they cross at the top. Lay a horizontal pole on the cross and tie together. Other pairs are pushed into the ground about 6 inches apart and tied into the top pole. The finished structure is surprisingly rigid, as it needs to be when a strong wind blows against the wall of foliage in summer.

There is a third technique, favoured by people like Poppy and Carlo, who use a no-dig system of cultivation. They put manure and compost on the ground in the autumn in rows, or circles in Poppy's case because she grows beans in a wigwam shape, and cover it with black plastic to encourage it to rot. When the plastic comes off at planting time, worms should have carried all the compost into the ground, where the bean roots can feed on it.

Once the runner-bean poles are up, I begin the whole process again for the French beans. It is harder work than it seems and I keep resisting the temptation to bring the deckchair out of the shed and take a breather in the warm sun because I know if I do, I won't start work again today. I might as well have done because I don't manage to finish the job before supper time. I cut a small spring cabbage to take with me together with a handful of baby sugar snap peas, which still have the withered blossoms at the ends. I picked two handfuls but couldn't resist eating half of them raw. They crunch in the mouth and burst with sweet juice, rather like a very crisp apple. Extremely moreish.

Thursday

Poppy is creating a nest of bent willow and raffia around the painted wooden owl which perches on top of a weatherbeaten post, overlooking the globe artichokes, as I pass. I am still aching from doing the beans yesterday, so I stop and ask her how the no-dig system works. I have never quite understood it.

'The preparation of the soil is vital,' she says. 'It must be dug over and over and cleaned of every bit of perennial weed and root. Sometimes I bend over a spadeful of soil a dozen times to pick everything out. Then you must make beds enclosed by planks or bricks which are no more than 4 feet wide, so you can reach everywhere without walking onto them, because that is vital, too. If you walk on the ground, you compress it, and then it has to be dug to open up the soil structure.'

'But surely weeds still grow on them,' I say. 'Seeds must blow in from elsewhere.'

'Annual weeds, yes. But they are no problem. You just pull them out by hand.'

'Doesn't the soil compact anyway over time, with the action of rain and sun?'

'It settles, but it doesn't get hard. Carlo and I haven't had to dig any of our beds for five years, and that is a great boon.'

'I bet.' I must think about switching to that system, but the initial digging and sifting of the soil sounds hard work. Maybe I could try it out with just one or two small beds to see how it works.

Further along, I stop in awe as I see the Ace Cultivator at work. He is doing something that I have only ever seen in illustrations in older gardening books, or demonstrated occasionally on television programmes more as a curiosity than as a recommended practice. He is double digging, and there is something almost mystical about it. Feel as if I am witnessing an ancient art thought to have been lost in the mists of time.

He has dug a trench from one side of the plot to the other which is 3 feet deep – I make him measure it for me. Into the bottom go barrowloads of fresh manure, on top of that goes back the subsoil and then the topsoil. It is finished off with more loads of well-rotted manure.

The trench will gradually move from one end of the area he is digging to the other. This raises the soil level by several inches, creates a greater depth of fertility, more room for roots to spread and improves drainage. An all-round very good thing, but incredibly hard work.

'I am deeply impressed,' I say. 'But also exhausted just looking at you. How many months will it take you to do the whole plot?'

'I just do a third of it a year, and only this plot, not the others. It does take a long time, but it's worth it. Everything grows so much better where I've done this.'

After that, finishing off my French bean trenches is like falling off a log. The dark shoots of the potatoes are through again and need further earthing up in case of frost. If the temperature drops to even a degree or so above freezing, they will shrivel, though the potatoes underneath will be all right and the shoots

soon recover. Notice that the fresh green leaves on the gooseberries are mottled with grey. A few of the berries are also
affected. I think this might be the dreaded American gooseberry
mildew which has given Alan next door so much trouble. He
gets it every year on his four large bushes and he talks about
uprooting and burning them, but never gets round to it.

The seven crowns of unforced rhubarb are growing vigorously, clearly benefiting from the stable manure I piled over
them in the autumn. I am really proud of these because I grew
them from seed a few years ago. Until I saw them in a seed catalogue, I had thought the only way to propagate rhubarb was by
sub-dividing crowns, and at the time I couldn't find any nearby
garden centre which sold crowns.

When I pull some stalks, I disturb two frogs which leap into
the frog pond with almost simultaneous splashes. The pond is
just a large plastic storage box, sunk into the ground between
two crowns where the broad leaves will shelter the water and
frogs in summer. It has a ramp of bricks and stone inside so
they can climb in and out easily. I encourage frogs because
they eat lots of slugs. Toads do, too, though the habitat they
like, a gently rotting woodpile, is slug heaven, so that is not so
good. I should put in a much larger pond, like the one Magic
has, and have fish and grow some water plants, but where
would I find the room? Perhaps I should think about getting
another allotment.

Thursday
Really warm, shirtsleeve weather today. Frightened twice by
bumblebees lurching into me as if drunk on sun or nectar. They
are like small, furry birds with a peevish, looking-for-a-fight
drone.

'Bzzz. Oy, get outta my way or else. Bzzz, hic.'

I don't know whether they have stings and I don't want to find
out from them, painfully, so I do get outta their way, fast. The
Brussels sprouts and broccoli have thrown up large clusters of
yellow flowers, which may be attracting the bees.

Saleem and Alan are standing beside one of Alan's ancient compost bins. He has removed the carpet which covered it. Just the man I want to see about my gooseberries. When I join them, they are gazing into the bin with expressions of rapt admiration.

'That's good,' says Saleem. 'How old is it?'

'Umm.' Alan screws his face up as thinks back. 'Oh, it must be at least five years.' Five-year-old compost! This is the equivalent of vintage port.

Saleem picks up a handful and sniffs it. 'Lovely stuff,' he says as if he wants to slap it between two slices of bread and eat it. Instead, he hands it on to me. It feels warm and has the texture and colour of coarse peat with nutty chocolate drops in it. It has a pleasant, slightly sweet, mushroomy smell.

Compost provokes a passion among some allotment folk that other people feel for football or their cars. If you want to make an enemy for life of an allotmenteer, criticise his or her compost. I don't really have the knack for it because I never have the patience to build a heap with the correct mixture of fine and coarse, woody and soft material in layers as the books advise. In real life such a variety of compostable material never presents itself all together. I also forget to turn the heap regularly. I still get reasonable results from muddling along, though nothing as good as this.

'Alan, will you look at my gooseberries?' I ask. He studies them, bending over with creaking difficulty to get a closer look.

'Yes, 'fraid so. That's the mildew all right, but it's very early.'

'It's the weather,' says Saleem gloomily. Though born in Trinidad, he does not like the heat and never dresses for it, wearing Wellington boots, long-sleeved woolly shirts and a hat even in August. 'It's too warm for April. It will bring everything on far too quickly and then there'll be a frost and we'll all be in trouble. I see your potatoes are through. You'd better cover them up with straw at night.' He goes off, muttering, 'At this rate we'll have a hosepipe ban by June.' He clearly has a problem with the weather.

Mildew. Damn. I'm sure I bought mildew-resistant bushes

because of Alan's trouble. I fetch a copy of Ken Muir's fruit guide from the shed and check the names of the bushes, Yellow Champagne and Lancashire Lad, which were bought at Wisley. They are not on his list of resistant varieties, and now I remember that the resistant ones they had were only suitable for cooking, so I didn't buy them. Double damn!

The contents of Tardis have sunk a couple of inches more, and there's another hole in the surface.

Cut half a dozen asparagus spears for supper, the first of the crop. I don't know why mine grow so much thicker than the ones in the shops. Perhaps I feed them too much. Every autumn I cover the bed with 6 inches of compost which has all gone by midsummer, dragged down by worms. At home, steam them and serve with butter and black pepper. Crooningly delicious – after every mouthful my wife and I close our eyes and croon: 'Oh, it's so good' – and so tender, despite their girth, that there is no wastage.

Saturday

The sun is blazing from a brilliant blue sky and by late morning the temperature is about 25 degrees Centigrade. I move into summer mode: shorts, T-shirt and beach shoes, which is a first for April and one in the eye for those scientists who still claim that global warming is a figment of other people's imaginations.

To the Hut to get something for the mildew. 'Hello, darling,' cries Queeny, who is just pouring water from the kettle into the pot. 'Want a cup of tea?'

'He'd rather have a cold beer,' says Sailor.

'Have you got one?' asks the Birdman, looking up so eagerly from measuring out the contents of various bins and drums into a bag that he catches his head on the seed-packet display and knocks it sideways. 'Bugger.'

'Beer?' mutters Five Pints, stirring behind the stack of fertiliser and lime sacks at the end of the Hut, where he has been taking a nap in the cool.

'I've got a problem,' I start. This is greeted with laughter and ribald remarks about my shorts. 'No, really. Mildew on the gooseberries. What do I do?'

Sailor raises a hand to silence everyone. 'Forget that lot.' He gestures at the shelves of chemical treatments behind him. 'The best thing is to spray with a solution of washing soda. That works, really it does. Repeat it every two weeks until the mildew is gone. It's also good for blackfly.'

'Washing soda?' I ask, genuinely puzzled. 'Wasn't that something my grandma used for clothes in the days of coal-fired washing coppers?'

'You can still get it in supermarkets,' says Queeny. It's worth a try. At worst, if it doesn't work, I will have the cleanest mildewy gooseberries on the allotments.

The Birdman hefts his bag on to the desk and prepares to pay for it.

'What's in that?' asks Sailor, who has to work out a price.

The Birdman tell him. 'It's a Special Mixture. I add this to the ground where I transplant seedlings from pots and it eases them in gently, without the shock of being moved, which can hold back growth for a week or more. Not for all of them – I couldn't afford that. It's just for the plants I reckon will have a chance in the show.'

Five Pints leans forward with sudden interest, revealing himself to the Birdman who didn't know he was there. I can see the dismay on his face as he realises he has given away one of his secrets to a rival. He thinks furiously and says: 'Of course, it won't work without a couple of other ingredients which I can't tell you about right now,' and looks daggers at Five Pints.

Sunday

I round up my younger boy and his friend to help me shift the bits of greenhouse. They ask: 'How much?' and when I make an offer they go into a huddle. 'For how long?'

Airily, I guess: 'Ooh, no more than an hour, probably a lot less.' They go into another huddle, then they state their terms. 'What?' I exclaim in outrage.

'Well, it is Sunday, and there are lots of other things we could be doing.' They have me over a barrel. There's a bank-holiday mood on the allotments. Families are picnicking in the sun, and every trip we make with the wheelbarrow to collect the green-house bits is interrupted at length by people wanting to chat. Halfway through the second-to-final trip the two boys down tools and ostentatiously look at their watches.

'The hour's up,' says the friend. 'You'll have to pay us over-time.' Where do teenage boys learn the hard-nosed negotiating skills of the Amalgamated Boilermaker's Union? I pay them off with a bad grace and they scarper. Something has happened to the greenhouse in the short journey from the Birdman's plot to mine. There, the parts looked like a dismantled greenhouse waiting to be put back together again. Here, they are an anony-mous jumble of glass and metal panels and struts. They could be anything – the debris of a plane crash, even. I'll never be able to assemble it. I half-heartedly try to fit one bit to another, turn them end to end and try again. It's no good. I haven't got a clue. I'll have to wait until the Birdman's in a good mood with half a day to kill and get him to show me. The parts will stay stacked against the sides of the tool locker and shed until then.

The Artist has set up an easel on the main path and is paint-ing a lilac tree. 'Isn't the weather lovely?' she says. She must have forgiven me for the peach.

Tuesday
It takes me a while to track down washing soda to an old-fashioned hardware store. A big box costs less than £1. Sailor didn't say how it should be diluted, and the manufacturers haven't had the foresight to print gardening instructions on the box, so I throw a handful into a half-gallon sprayer and shake it up. When I have given the gooseberries a good soaking, the sprayer is still three-quarters full, so I do the red- and blackcur-rants. There is still plenty left, and I think if it works against mildew, it may also prevent blight and leaf curl so I give the peach and gages and raspberries a preventative shower until it

has all gone. By now the spray has dried on the gooseberries, leaving the leaves coated with white. Oh, dear. I must have used too strong a solution. I remember Grandma saying soap and water never hurt anything when I shrieked loudly as she lathered my five-year-old ears. I just hope gooseberry leaves are as resilient as boys' ears.

Friday
The enchanting sight of a full moon in a cloudless sky on a still night makes me pause before drawing the bedroom curtains just before midnight. The opening lines of the poem 'Silver' by Walter de la Mare come back to me from schooldays:

> Slowly, silently now the moon
> Walks the night in her silver shoon.

Magical.

> This way and that, she peers and sees
> Silver fruit upon silver trees.

But wait a minute. Where's that black smoke coming from? A thick column of it is rising up over the rooftops, as if intent on blotting the moon out. As I watch, the base of the column glows red and begins to flicker with flames.

For a moment I am seized by an ancient dread of fire, springing up out of control, all consuming and terrifying in its blind destructiveness. Then I am running downstairs, out through the door and along the deserted streets. By the time I reach the allotment gates, there is a distant wail of sirens and I leave the gates open so the fire engine can follow me in.

A group of sheds is burning with steady ferocity, flames roaring up into the night. Well-seasoned timber, paraffin and garden chemicals make a highly flammable mixture. The heat ignites a compost heap and a couple of large stacks of straw. The fire engine has to stop at the gates because its way is blocked by rubbish skips. The firemen unroll their hoses but they don't reach even quarter of the way. I point out the standpipes and they attach hoses to them. They are dry. The water supply should have been switched on a couple of weeks ago, but it has been delayed because some leaking pipes need to be repaired.

The firemen refuse to give in. They collect whatever containers they can find in the dark – buckets, bottles, plant pots – and scoop up water from tanks and butts and throw it on the flames. In other circumstances, in a television comedy sketch, it would have been funny to see these big men in helmets and protective clothing carrying little pots of water almost daintily across the allotments to try to douse the fire. But this is not make-believe.

Nothing is saved. The sheds and their contents are totally destroyed. I ask the fire chief what he thinks had happened. 'Definitely malicious,' he says. 'That straw had me worried. If the wind had been blowing the half-gale it was the day before yesterday, burning straw could have been blown on to those houses there and fire could have taken hold while the occupants slept. That would have been disastrous.'

Feel sure we are being watched. The arsonists are hiding in the dark among the allotments exulting at the drama they have created, and they are about to strike again.

Saturday
Wisps of smoke are still rising from the ruins of two more sheds when I arrive at 10.30 a.m., and then I see the greatest outrage of all. The Birdman's greenhouse has been burned to the ground. That is not all. It was stuffed to the roof with trays and pots of seedlings, hundreds of things including much of his stock of competition-standard onions, sweet peas, dahlias and chrysanthemums. All gone.

'How?' I ask, as I look at the twisted aluminium spars, the shattered glass, the scraps of melted plastic and the piles of blackened soil. 'How can a greenhouse burn down?'

For the first time since I have known him, the Birdman has

lost his jaunty, cheerful manner. His face is grey and his shoulders are hunched as if he has a pain in the chest. He has just returned from taking Molly home in tears. Her distress was all the greater for knowing that the fire must have terrified their caged birds and animals, only a few feet away.

When he answers, his voice is hoarse. 'Plastic. It was still lined with bubble wrap for insulation. They stacked straw bales against it as well, and the planks I use for walking on the beds.'

'But why?' Why did the vandals pick such an unlikely target as a greenhouse, when a few feet to one side is a big shed with timber piled against it and on the other a wooden aviary? He shakes his head and shudders, unable to fathom the minds of such barbarians and unwilling to think about the awfulness of his birds and rabbits being burned alive.

Everyone is stunned by the attack. Some people talk about gangs of drunken youths marauding about the allotments after dark who assault anyone who challenges them, but I am not clear whether this is fact or fear-fuelled fantasy. Everyone feels vulnerable and some of the older and frailer allotmenteers say they don't want to come any more, which is tragic.

Then, like any robust community which is under attack, people rally and draw together for self-defence. A dozen of us gather in the public bar of the Fox and Ferret to discuss what we can do. We will ask the police to advise us on security, and the Hon. Sec. drafts a letter to the council demanding it does something about its long-term neglect of the allotment fences. There is talk of vigilante patrols, but we settle for drawing up a notice advising people on precautions they can take to minimise damage. The hard truth is that the allotments cannot be made vandal-proof, and the only help we can expect is the help we provide ourselves. Despite meeting in the pub, we are a very sober group when the meeting breaks up.

Tuesday
I am astonished. The Birdman, jaunty and cheerful once more, is erecting the frame of another greenhouse which someone has given him. It is old and battered, but he has a genius for making things fit together and he is not short of helpers. There is also a constant stream of people bringing pots of seedlings to replace the ones he has lost.

I give him some of the onion seedlings, a giant variety, that I am growing for the autumn show – ironically, to challenge his supremacy in that class. It will be a fascinating contest now between plants with an identical start but raised by different people.

The vandals might burn and wreck our property, but they will not break our spirit. Out of the ashes a phoenix is rising.

May

'It's a grand morning,' says the Ace Cultivator. It is. Quite wonderful. The sort of morning you want to take a slice of and
preserve to bring out in the depths of winter. He raises a finger
and says in a stage whisper: 'If you stand still for a moment, you
can hear the plants growing.'

I think if I stood still for half a minute, I would actually see
them growing, but there is no time for idleness today. There is
too much to do. Runner beans to train up poles, French beans to
plant out, broad beans to stop, planting mounds to build for

courgettes and beds to prepare for sweetcorn and tomatoes, and a dozen other things.

Despite all this, I allow Magic to waylay me further up the path. Why am I so easily distracted? I think that secretly I must just want to enjoy the day for its own sake. He is leaning with clasped hands on his hoe and as I come up to him he says, 'Where have all the sparrows gone?' He is gazing off towards the unruly hedge along the railway cutting. At intervals along the hedge are several tall trees, which have been separately colonised by starlings, magpies and crows. Now he mentions it, I cannot remember the last time I saw a house or hedge sparrow here, though I see them in the garden at home in groups of up to eight, squabbling over bread crusts thrown on the lawn.

He goes on: 'There used to be lots of them. I put up three nesting boxes for sparrows a few months ago and not one has been used. I saw blue tits looking inside, but they haven't nested in them either.'

'You hardly ever see blackbirds now,' I say. 'There used to be lots of them, too, and I don't think I've seen a thrush for about three years. Are they being poisoned by slug pellets or something?'

He shakes his head. 'It's the magpies. They raid nests and eat eggs and chicks. Have you noticed how many there are around here now? Hundreds of them. And as they have increased, all the other birds, especially the songbirds, have decreased.'

There are certainly far more magpies about than there used to be. Only pigeons are more numerous. They are birds of field and wood which never used to be seen much in the suburbs. Perhaps they have moved here to get away from persecution by country people, who consider them vermin and birds of ill omen, to be shot at any opportunity.

My superstitious mother always quotes the rhyme about magpies if she sees one – *One for sorrow* – and will not rest until she sees a second to cancel out that curse – *Two for joy*. After glimpsing a solitary bird in a field, she has been known to make my father drive up and down a country lane for twenty minutes in increasing agitation until she has seen another. *Three for a girl, four for a boy. Five for silver, six for gold. Seven for a secret never to be told.* What about eight, or does it stop there?

I counted nineteen magpies in an allotment apple tree last November, with two crows at the very top. They perched quietly while the crows called back and forth. What was going on there? When I told Alan about it, he said that size of gathering by magpies was called a parliament, though he had no idea why they collect in such numbers.

When I get to my plot and lift the lid of the Tardis to add a bag of peelings, two mice are sitting on the top. All three of us freeze. They have been eating bread and stare at me in open-mouthed, twitching-nosed shock, as I would if a giant suddenly took the ceiling off my dining room in the middle of lunch. They must be wood mice because they are noticeably bigger than house mice, with thick grey coats and larger eyes and ears. They dive for cover and vanish down two holes. There are eight holes altogether, and the compost has sunk a third of the way down the bin.

Now I know why it has been shrinking faster than I can top it up. I had fondly thought it was because it was rotting down so well. No: it has been eaten. This is not a compost bin at all. It is a five-star hotel and restaurant for mice. I happily accept the loss of a fair amount of crops to wildlife as the price of sharing the land with them, but this is too much. The mice have to go.

I find several holes burrowed under the skirt of the Tardis at ground level which I had not noticed before, and stop them up with bits of plank to prevent more mice getting in. I have been so sidetracked today that I have not managed to plant the French beans or do half the things I meant to.

Thursday
I get stung twice on the left leg just below the knee as I kneel on the ground in shorts to train the runner beans. They were so sharp that I thought it was thorns or wasps, but when I stretch

out my leg I see it is red ants. There are nests of them all over the allotment and at this time of year they sting very readily. By tonight I will have two dark-red patches the size of small coins which will be itchy for days.

'No time for sitting in the sun,' chides Saleem, coming on to the plot.

I point at my leg. 'Ant bites.'

He peers at the skin but there is nothing to see yet. 'Put vinegar on them. Or lemon juice.' He looks around the plot, nodding his head slowly, which could indicate approval or confirmation of his worst fears. 'Those potatoes are well on.'

'Aren't they?' I say with pride.

'You planted them far too early. Why?'

I am suddenly put on the defensive. 'Because the sprouts were growing so long they either had to go in the ground or go to the barbers. Anyway, the weather was warm.'

'Look. There and there.' Where he points I see slight crinkling and browning at the edge of leaves on the lush growth. 'That's cold damage. Don't be fooled by the noon-day sun. At five in the morning it's damned cold here. Every night the cold goes pinch, pinch, and sets them back a little.'

'But what else could I have done?'

'Next year, if they are sprouting too fast, put them somewhere cool like the shed to slow them down. Cover them up now with that straw you have over there.'

'What, now, in May?'

'If you don't want to lose them.' As Saleem was one of the top prizewinners at last year's show and knows what he is talking about, I meekly do as I am told. 'When the frost danger is past, pull the straw down from the leaves into the trenches, where it will act as a mulch to hold in moisture.' Yes, sir. Then he sees my garlic and stops in admiration. The green, chive-like leaves, are tall and straight and vigorous.

'They're nice, very nice,' he says, beaming at me. 'Water them well until the bulbs start to swell, then stop. If you water them after that, the fibrous roots will rot away and the bulbs will go slimy and lose their protective paper skins which will let in eelworm and rot.' He gives the plot a last perusal and says: 'You're doing good.' I feel really pleased.

Go to the hardware shop on the way home to buy three wooden mousetraps, a design called The Little Nipper, to set up inside the Tardis, though not yet. There is so much mouse food in there that they are unlikely to be lured into traps smelling of humans. I will wait a few days until everything has gone rotten and store kitchen waste at home in a plastic sack for now.

In the meantime I will leave the lid off the bin in the hope that nature will exert a bit of its own control, and just to make it easier I lean a plank against the rim so that hungry foxes and cats can climb up there. There are also a couple of kestrels around hunting for mice, and maybe an owl.

Friday

The treachery of spring. With everything indicating that summer had already arrived, gloriously early, disaster struck last night out of a clear sky. A killer frost has massacred the darling buds of May.

It came like a thief in the night, stealthily and without warning. By the time I get down to the allotments in mid-morning, people are standing around treasured plants in twos and threes, pointing damage out to each other and offering sympathy. The frost came at the worst possible time, when all the fruit had set and was beginning to form. By all accounts it was very light, just on freezing or at the most a degree below, yet it has done immense damage. What has shocked people most is the capriciousness of the frost. Plants thought to be semi-hardy have been killed, in some cases the first frost casualties of their type in memory, while other plants known to be tender and growing almost alongside the victims have been spared.

The Ace Cultivator says: 'This is a terrible sight,' before pushing aside the tops of his gooseberry bushes to show me the ground underneath covered in berries already turning brown. 'I would have started to pick the first of these next week.'

'Have any survived?' I ask.

'A few, yes. Strangely, the ones which were most ripe. You'd think they would be the first to go because they have the highest moisture content.'

'Unless the sugar in the juice stopped it freezing.'

'That's a thought,' he says. 'Look at the peaches and plums. Decimated.'

Magic seems to have lost about half his cherries. The tiny fruitlets have blackened on the stalk. Again, the survivors are the largest ones. Poppy is mourning her asparagus, which has collapsed on the ground like green worm casts. Everywhere the tops of potatoes have been blasted and the flowers on broad beans nipped off. One allotmenteer has lost an entire cold-frame of tomato plants, about a hundred of them.

I see all this on the way to my plot, and with every step up the inclined path my anxiety rises. What scene of devastation will greet me? I stop on the Ridgeway and take a deep breath. The old raspberry canes are closest to me and I see that some of the early fruit has been blackened, but only here and there. All the potato leaves which were not completely covered by the straw have been shrivelled. When I lift the straw, I find that the leaves underneath are fine. What a relief. Thank you, Saleem, for nagging me.

My asparagus has gone the way of Poppy's, but the beans are all right, which surprises me as they are very tender. Even more surprising, the fruitlets on the peach and greengages seem to be unharmed. They are growing on the south side of the wooden trellis, which must have protected them from the frost as it crept in from the north and east. It must also have protected the beans, several feet further into the plot but still in the lee of the trellis.

I have got off amazingly lightly. The trellis helped a lot, but I think another factor is that I am on a plateau and the frost rolled away down the incline towards the gate, damaging the plots of Magic, Poppy, Ace and others on the way.

May

Saturday
As tea circulates among a dozen or so allotmenteers in the Hut, the damage is being totted up with much shaking of heads and many deep sighs.

'Thanks,' I say to Saleem. 'You saved my chips. If it wasn't for you, I would have lost all my potato tops. How did you know it was coming?'

'I didn't. I was just being cautious.' He said the early-evening weather news on Thursday had predicted an overnight temperature a few degrees above freezing, but by mid-evening this had been revised down to between zero and minus one, and he had come out with a torch and sheets of newspaper and plastic to cover what he could. Others either did not see the later forecast or thought their plants would survive such a light frost, as the warm ground would radiate heat.

Everyone has lost something, especially fruit. More than half the peaches and plums were killed and much of the currants and raspberries. Apples and pears seem to have fared better, but more serious damage may become apparent later in the season. What grieves people is that there is no possibility of recovery. Fruit trees and bushes will not put out more blossom until next year.

Vegetables were not so badly affected, and the plants which were damaged, like asparagus and potatoes, will grow back, or, in the case of beans and tomatoes, they can be replaced with fresh stock. The Birdman had just bought in £40 worth of new chrysanthemums and has lost the lot. He is surprisingly philosophical about it considering what he had already lost in the fire. He says: 'There's no point complaining in gardening. Who's going to listen to you? You've just got to take the rough with the smooth.'

There are several theories about why such a light frost should cause so much damage. The most sensible comes from Middy, who says: 'There was a cold wind that night which carried the frost into areas which would normally be protected, like the middle of my gooseberry bushes.'

83

The weirdest is from the Ace Cultivator. 'That might account for some damage,' he concedes, 'but I think the plants were caught off guard. The unusually hot weather in April had lulled them into thinking summer was here and they had grown so quickly they were psychologically unable to withstand the shock of the cold.'

Silence falls as people mull this over. Plants not only thinking but being capable of entering a psychological state is a radical and rather unsettling idea. One or two puzzled glances come Ace's way, as if to wonder if he is turning into a New Ager who will start telling us that carrots have feelings, too, you know.

'Well,' I say, to get the conversation going again, 'I have never known a frost as late as this.'

'I have,' says Brutally Frank. 'The year the Queen was crowned – 1953, wasn't it? – there was frost in June. And, to be brutally frank, this one is nothing compared to that. All the fruit was lost that year.'

Sunday

At long last it rains. At the first pattering of raindrops I want to rush outside and be soaked to enjoy the novelty of it. Then my new-found caution about the weather, learned the hard way, prevails. The moment I am soaked the temperature will plummet and I will be turned to ice, or lightning will strike me down.

Monday

More rain overnight and this morning. The ground soaks it up without puddling. I set the traps in the Tardis after giving a lot of thought to bait. What would entice mice in the midst of this half-rotten banquet? They are an unhealthy bunch, preferring chips to pasta and white bread to wholemeal. The scraps of chocolate croissants drive them wild. There is a plump sultana on one trap, a piece of bacon rind on another and, as someone at home ate the square of chocolate intended for the third, a chunk of my favourite Stilton cheese for that. I put the lid back on after counting twelve mouse holes in the top.

As I work, my eyes keep drifting towards the compost bin, and I keep fancying I hear the snap of traps. After twenty minutes, I give in and lift the lid. There are dead mice in two of the traps, but not the one with the Stilton. I throw the mice on the ground for the foxes and rebait the traps.

I check again an hour later, just before I leave, and the Stilton has caught one. The Tardis must be heaving with mice.

Tuesday

Yesterday's discarded mice have disappeared and all three traps are full again. Reset them and put out fresh bait of sultanas. Weeds are springing up after the rain and I spend an hour hoeing. Pick a yellowing gooseberry and eat it. Lovely, fully deserving the name of Yellow Champagne. My berries survived the frost and the washing soda seems to have done the trick of clearing mildew from the leaves. I underplanted the bushes with lettuces, which are being badly eaten by slugs, though they haven't touched the rocket nearby. Slugs have become much more active since the recent rain. Pick more gooseberries and offer a couple to Confucius as he comes by with the comment that these may be the only ones he'll taste this year, given their rarity value. 'Mmm, mmm,' he sighs. There is no higher praise.

Confucius returns later with a bunch of spinach leaves for me. He holds one up and turns it this way and that so that, even on an overcast day, the buttery green catches the light and glows like smoked glass. Popeye would drool at the sight. I love spinach but rarely grow it because no one else in the family will eat it. I tried to smuggle it into the children's food when they were younger, but they always spotted it and shoved it to the side of their plates, saying 'Yuk' and 'Ugh'.

Wednesday

Try to pinch out the growing tips of sweet peas under the trellis, but it is an awkward job and give up when I feel I may be inadvertently taking off too much and doing more harm than good. Wander over to see Middy, who is dropping peas into an inch of

paraffin in a jam jar. 'None of the peas I planted months ago have come up,' she says. 'It wasn't wet enough to make them rot, so they must have been eaten by mice.'

'There's an awful lot of them around,' I say with feeling, and tell her about the Tardis.

'This will stop them.' After a minute of swirling she takes the lid off the jar and pours the excess paraffin back into a can. 'The trick is to soak them long enough to take on the smell, but not so long that the paraffin goes through the skin and kills the pea.' She bends over to tip the peas into a seed tray on the ground to dry. It is warm again today and she is wearing very short shorts and a halter top.

'Tricky,' I say. Back at the plot, I decide to uncover the potatoes in the belief that there will be no more frost. The potatoes are taking the decision for themselves. They are growing so fast after the rain that they have pushed the straw aside. I do as Saleem said and pull it down into the trenches, meaning to damp it down with a weak solution of pelleted chicken manure in water to encourage it to rot.

'What are you growing there?' asks the Birdman from the Ridgeway.

'These are Charlotte second earlies.

He comes over to look at them. 'In Ireland, where I come from, as I've probably told you, and where people know a thing or two about them, a potato is a potato is a potato. There's none of this palaver about first earlies and second earlies and salad potatoes and main crops.

'Let me tell you, an early potato is simply a spud that is planted sooner than the rest and harvested while it is still small and sweet. Leave it in the ground another month and, hey presto, it becomes a second early. Leave it till September and it's a main crop.' He beckons me closer with a crooked fore-finger as if he is going to impart something confidential he doesn't want overheard, though there is no one else within shouting distance.

'I had a whole lot of so-called first earlies left over, and I was giving them away to anyone who wanted them. A woman from over thataways looked at them and turned up her nose and asked if I had any second earlies. I tried to tell her what I've just told you and she wouldn't have any of it. She had to have second earlies.' He stops talking for a second and a slow, mischievous smile spreads across his face. 'So I said, "Come back tomorow, love, and I'll have some for you." I took the labels off the first earlies and gave them to her and, oh, she was grateful. She's growing them as second earlies and will never know the difference. Never in a million years.' He laughs.

More mice in the traps.

Thursday
Rita brings round a plug tray of mixed spring cabbage, broccoli, cauliflower and Brussels sprout seedlings which she has left over. I wasn't planning to grow any more brassicas for next spring because there is no space left now that I have planted so much

fruit. But I can't say no to such a kindness, and I accept them. I will have to find room between the beds and along edges.

'You know that Victoria plum you were asking for?' she says. Saleem has a magnificent Victoria on his plot beside the railway cutting with the habit of throwing up suckers from its roots which rapidly become saplings. Half the plum trees growing on the allotments have come from this tree, and I have been pestering him for one. 'He says he has one ready for you if you come to the Hut on Saturday. Only he said you have to be prepared to . . .'. She glances over my shoulder and stops talking as a look of horror crosses her face. I whip round.

Middy is coming down the path towards us in those tight shorts and a T-shirt looking like a modern-day Medusa, for she is holding out a handful of squirming snakes.

'Oh my God,' mutters Rita. She has gone pale. I probably have, too, and I take a step back.

Middy says: 'Do any of you want one?' as nonchalantly as if she is offering a radish or a spring onion. We both shake our heads. 'Slow worms,' she says. 'I found two nests of them when I moved the carpet off my compost and I am spreading them around. They are very good for eating slugs and woodlice.' We nod with strained smiles as we would to a mad bag lady who had accosted us on the high street and back away. The slow worms wriggle and squirm horribly.

Friday
Poppy says accusingly: 'I hear you have been catching a lot of mice in your shed.' She is against killing anything, except slugs, and then only in a humane fashion.

'Not in the shed,' I say in my defence, though the mice have eaten all the packets of green manure seed in there. 'In the compost bin. It's riddled with them.'

'They don't do any real harm, do they?' It is less of a question than a statement.

I remember that Poppy puts out food for foxes, which infuriates the people who consider them vermin. 'They eat the compost which I need to feed my plants, so I catch them and feed them to the foxes. That seems an organic approach to pest control.'

I don't think she agrees with that, but then I don't think I do either. I have been feeling more and more uneasy about trapping all those mice, and last night I dreamed I was eating a sandwich filled with mouse tails. When I lift the lid of the Tardis there are two mice in traps. I have now caught seventeen of them.

What makes me uneasy is the feeling that I am killing mice for behaving like mice in a place which is as much theirs as it is mine. They are only doing what comes naturally to them in natural surroundings. It is not as if they are playing havoc in my kitchen or running across the bedroom floor. I clear the traps and drop them into a plastic bag which I put in a corner of the shed out of the way. From now on, mice can eat as much of my compost as they like. In fact, I've noticed they only eat food which is relatively fresh. Once things get really mouldy they don't touch them.

Saturday
'This one,' asks Saleem, 'or that one?' The first sucker branches low down and is bushy. The second is taller with a central stem which divides halfway up into three erect branches. I choose that one. There are many more smaller ones in a ragged circle around the parent tree. As Saleem digs it up he says: 'They be vigorous and fruitful. Have you seen the Ace Cultivator's?' I nod. He has several, pruned into neat bushes 7 feet tall, which produce heavy crops of mouth-watering fruit. 'They started this size, three, four years ago. But they'll grow bigger than his if you let them. See Gran'pappy there.' He indicates the original tree, which has a dense, spreading canopy, most of it far too high to harvest without a ladder.

I have already dug the planting hole at the end of a row of blackcurrant bushes. On the other side of the hole is the path in front of the compost bins. I half fill the hole with ancient compost and spread over it what roots the sapling has – not many. Then I fill the rest of the hole with topsoil.

'It's a good spot,' says Saleem. 'Plenty of light and far enough from the main path so that people passing along won't be able to pinch the fruit.'

'Rita was starting to tell me the other day that I had to be prepared for something, but she never said what.'

'Didn't I tell you? It'll probably die.'

'What?' I exclaim.

'Not probably. Maybe,' he corrects himself. 'You should really transplant them in the dormant season. Now he's got a lot of leaf on him and the shock of moving will be greater. But you were so eager to have him that I thought it was worth the risk.'

'But if it's going to die . . .'

'Now, don't go upsetting yourself. Give him a lot of water, often, and he might be all right. If not, I'll give you another in the autumn.'

Friday

There is a very good turnout for the last talk of the lecture programme. By the time I arrive, ten minutes before the talk starts, the church hall is already full and noisy and it looks as if it might be standing room only. The Hon. Sec. has brought two buckets of his home-made wine – the pink, sweetish one made from a mixture of summer fruit – and it is going so fast he may have to fetch more supplies. People not familiar with his sometimes potent brews are drinking it by the mugful because it tastes like fruit squash. Wait till they try to stand up to go home.

The subject of the talk is 'Growing Vegetables For Show', given by a leading local judge of horticultural shows. The posters say he will be revealing the secrets of the show bench and giving tips on how to win prizes, which explains his popularity. He arrives and there is a scramble for seats. More chairs are brought in from the church, and I have to make do with one behind the slide projector.

The judge is introduced and there is a reverential hush. He is big and square and ruminative, from a bygone age before television gave gardening a sexy make-over, when experts always seemed to be men called Bert, Sid, Stan or Ted, who wore a collar and tie whatever the weather and whatever the work. I just know that every word he utters will be worth its weight in gold and I have brought pen and paper to write them down.

'What judges look for in exhibits are freshness, straightness, freedom from blemishes, clear skins, uniformity and, where appropriate, an inch of stalk to show that they haven't been bought from a shop.' As he speaks pictures come up on the screen of perfect produce perfectly displayed on show benches.

'Now, I can hear you thinking, "He's asking a lot", especially when it come to trying to match a pair of vegetables, or in the case of beans and peas, maybe as many as nine pods, which are growing at different rates.' He points to the screen. "How can I get exhibits looking as good as that?" you're asking. Well, I'll tell you.' There is a quickening of interest in the room. Other people are also writing busily.

'If you want beans which are straight, tie a weight to the bottom. As they reach exhibition size – and remember they must be flat with no beany bulges – pick them, cover in cling film and put them in the fridge. They will keep in good condition like that for a couple of weeks.

'Grow carrots and parsnips in 40-gallon drums or in pipes filled with a 60:40 mix of sand and soil.' I glance over at the Birdman, who is looking distinctly unhappy at the outing of his secret. 'If a show class calls for a pair of something, you can be sure uniformity is essential. To achieve that with marrows, for example, one which is ready can be cut and kept in a fridge like the beans while another one catches up. On exhibition day recut the stalk of the first one so it appears fresh.'

'An almost-guaranteed way of getting a batch of potatoes of uniform appearance is to grow them in 10-inch pots filled with a growbag mix and with straw at the bottom. Cut the tops off a week before the show so the skins will toughen and not rub off with handling. If insects have made holes in the potatoes, fill them with soap.' All over the room heads are bowed over pens scratching furiously on paper. I keep missing the slides because I want to get every word down.

'Don't think you can fool judges by entering onions grown from sets in classes for onions grown from seed, and vice versa. Set-grown onions have bigger, slightly corky base plates.' I never knew that.

'To get nice even tomatoes, restrict the plant to four or five trusses.' The judge then gives a list of the best vegetable varieties for exhibition purposes which seems to be all about size and uniformity. I have never heard of most of them. The applause at the end of the talk is thunderous. He has clearly given people what they wanted to hear.

Over the road in the Fox and Ferret I reflect that the criteria for shows is all, well, show. Appearance for appearance's sake.

'I was going to raise that very point,' says the Ace Cultivator.

'A 3-foot leek looks very impressive on the bench,' I say. 'But I bet it's so tough it's probably inedible.'

The Hon. Sec. says: 'The trouble is, how can you judge for taste and flavour – except in the obvious cases of chutneys and jams and tarts.'

'They could make a start with fruit,' says Middy. 'I've never seen a judge nibble a strawberry or an apple.'

The Birdman says morosely: 'That won't work for carrots or tatties, and you can't show a dish of cooked ones.' He is really put out about the carrot and parsnip tip being made public – Five Pints is looking quietly pleased with himself.

'I still think,' I say, 'that show rules are getting the priorities wrong. They are losing sight of the most important factor for all of us, which is that we grow things to eat, and how they taste is what matters above everything.' Glasses around the table are raised to that sentiment. I don't say what really worries me: that after that talk the competition at our next show in September is going to be razor sharp.

June

Monday

I can smell summer. I notice it as soon as I open the gates and the smell gets stronger as I walk further into the site. I stop on the Ridgeway and take a couple of deep, slow breaths. Mmm. The air is a cocktail of delicious scents. There must be hundreds of them, mostly unidentifiable. Yesterday it was still spring and today, with identical weather, it is summer, so what has made the difference?

I take another breath and let it out slowly. I can't tell, but I think something has happened similar to when you make a casserole and all the ingredients in the pot keep their individual smells or tastes until a critical moment in the cooking when they merge and create a new aroma. Summer is a-cooking.

The sky is full of swifts darting and swooping after insects. They must be a couple of hundred feet high, yet their twittering calls are quite distinct. I watch their aerial ballet for a while and wonder what insects are doing so high in the air when nearly all of them feed down here on my plants.

Saleem's sapling is wilting. The leaves are limp when I touch them. This may be because the roots have not had time to settle in and cannot supply enough moisture to the leaves. Perhaps I should have removed half the leaves to reduce the demand, though the shock of that coming on top of the trauma of being uprooted might have killed it. I soak the ground around the sapling with two buckets of water and then fetch half a barrow-load of wood chips from where they have been dumped near the gates and spread it around the trunk as a thick mulch to stop the water from evaporating.

I should thin out the swelling fruit on the peach and green-gage trees, but put it off because there is always a natural fall of immature fruit in June and they are not overburdened. The leaves on the peach are long and narrow and a very glossy green, rather like sweet bay. The trees probably need water, too, and if I'm going to do them, I may as well do all the fruit. Get the hose out of the shed and set it up, which takes time because it is so twisted up. I always put it away neatly after use, looping it between thumb and elbow, and it has always uncoiled into knots when I go to fetch it again. It must be the same gremlin which makes sure that Christmas fairy lights, put away in full working order in January, are fused and dead when they are got out again in December.

It takes an hour and a half to give the plot a good soaking because the tap here is nearly at the end of the pipeline and pressure is low. Still, it gives me the perfect excuse to stand and stare and enjoy the sun. After the fruit, the vegetables. The onions are filling out nicely, but the bed is very weedy and they hate the competition because their roots don't go down far. I will have to hoe between the rows after this. The garlic leaves are yellowing. Saleem comes up the path shaking his head at me. 'What did I tell you about watering the garlic?'

'Um, er . . .'

'You must stop after the bulbs start to swell in May, otherwise they will rot. That's why they are turning yellow. If you dig up one you'll see that it's gone slimy because it's sitting in wet soil.' I drop the hose in among the beans and pull up one of the garlic heads. The leaves break off. I brush aside the wood-chip mulch and push my fingers into the earth and bring up an undersized bulb, which is, as Saleem said, slimy and horrible. Damn!

'Don't water them any more,' he says, 'and they should recover. How is the plum doing?'

'Not well,' I say, and show him.

He pulls a face. 'Keep giving it water and it may be all right.' He doesn't sound convinced. Plant the sweetcorn, which I have grown in the cardboard tubes saved from rolls of lavatory paper because they are as fussy as sweet peas about being transplanted and hate their roots to be disturbed. The tubes provide plenty of depth for the roots to develop, and once in the ground will go soggy so the roots can penetrate the sides. Plant them in saucer-shaped depressions which will hold water.

Tuesday

Cut ten spears of asparagus, some still as thick as the handle on my trowel but about half only the width of my index finger. This will be the last harvest, and I will now let the plants grow to produce their delicate ferny leaves and build themselves up for next year. They soon recovered from the frost damage last month, but the crowns are not very productive at the best of times and every year I think about digging them up and using the ground for something else. Then I taste them and they are reprieved.

When I start to pick the broad beans, I see the main stems of the plants and the stalks of the pods are covered by blackfly. I should have pinched out the growing tips last month – that is what they are attracted to. It's too late now. I will fetch some washing-up liquid from home and spray them with a strong solution. The flies weaken the plants by sucking sap and though this may prevent some flowers from setting and reduce the crop, they don't damage the pods or the beans inside them. Which means that I have been less vigilant than I should. What I have overlooked is the risk of the blackfly spreading to other plants, where they may do much more damage.

After picking half a bagful of pods my hands are stained black by squashed flies and I rinse them off in the water tank before harvesting anything else. The water is warm and soft and it takes some vigorous rubbing to remove the oily stains. Pick sugar snap peas, radishes, lettuces, spring onions, gooseberries, rhubarb and raspberries, then two huge bunches of sweet peas in white and soft shades of pink, blue and red.

Should I lift some potatoes? Decide not, mainly because I would have too much to carry, but carefully scrape the soil away from a plant to check on its progress. Three of the tubers are golf-ball sized and the others like grapes, so they are nearly ready for eating. Go home laden down with good things for tonight's supper, walking every step in a cloud of intoxicating perfume from the sweet peas. The flowers fill half a dozen vases which my wife puts in the kitchen, hall, sitting room, and bedrooms, and by evening the house is full of scent.

Wednesday
Put in a dozen tomato plants – Gardener's Delight, an Italian plum-shaped variety given to me by the Hon. Sec. which he thinks is called Roma, and Ailsa Craig. They are staked and have the pot they were raised in sunk into the soil around them so that water put in that will go directly to their roots instead of running away over the surface. I plant them on the corner furthest from the shed where the soil is poor. It reminds me that I should have started my home-made fertiliser production line a month ago when the comfrey began to bush up.

Russian comfrey was introduced into Britain in the nine-teenth century by Henry Doubleday, who believed that as a prolific source of protein and essential minerals, it was a plant which could save the world. This may have been overstating its importance, but it is invaluable to the organic gardener. A comfrey plant will last twenty years, producing a dense bush of leaves which, when cut, decompose rapidly to produce a thick black liquid. This contains a higher proportion of nitrogen, phosphorous and potassium than farm manure, as well as a score of other minerals, and all in a form which is instantly available to plants when added to the soil.

Comfrey plants produce a huge amount of leaf, several pounds per harvest, and they grow back so quickly that a plant can be cut every five or six weeks through the summer. I take the pruning knife out of my pocket and cut all six plants at ground level. There is a mound of leaves which fills an old rubbish bin on the far side of the allotment near the tomatoes. Before putting a slab of wood on top, weighted down with a brick, to compress them, I pour a bottle of old comfrey juice over the leaves to help start the process. Manage to splash my hands and shirt. The leaves will start to liquefy in days, and within a month will produce about a gallon and a half of fertiliser which I will dilute with ten times its volume of water before use.

There is just one drawback, which is why the bin is where it is. The liquid stinks so badly that it can be mistaken for sewage and attracts the sort of flies which like a good dung heap. But it is worth it because it is free as well as being so good.

The level of compost inside the Tardis has not dropped any more and the contents are thoroughly mouldy. I stir it around with a garden fork and reckon that it may be ready to use in a few weeks.

The cat-shaped wind vane on top of Magic's cherry tree, made out of a sheet of polystyrene, has swung round from the east to the south-west while I have been busy. The wind vane is also supposed to keep birds away from the cherries but the starlings which throng in the tree at this time of year have worked out that real cats don't sit in the air. Magic comes along and shoos them gently away.

He sniffs. 'That's powerful stuff you have there.'

'Yes, sorry about that,' I say, and to change the subject tell him about the Tardis.

He says: 'I have a colony of white mice living under my shed. I leave them be. I don't think they do any harm.'

'White mice?' I exclaim. 'How did they get there?'

'They must have been pets which escaped from one of the nearby houses. Or they might have been released here by someone who had got fed up with them. People have been known to throw unwanted pets over the fence.'

'Like what?' My mind is running away with images of monkeys and baby alligators. Fanciful, I know.

'Snakes.' He sees my shocked expression. 'Oh, yes, snakes. And other things.' He rolls his eyes and shudders. 'I hate snakes.' I daren't ask what the 'other things' might be.

Thursday

There are two other excellent organic fertilisers: seaweed extract, which is bought in concentrated form in bottles and is very expensive if used on a large scale, and pelleted chicken manure. This also has to be bought, usually in 5-kilo drums, and would be moderately expensive if used as dry pellets scattered around plants. Instead, acting on Sailor's advice that it is far too strong to be used neat, I put a small handful into a 2-gallon bucket, stir until it has dissolved and then pour it around plants needing lots of nitrogen, which is most leafy things. Used in this way, a drum of pellets will last two seasons and each watering canful will have cost a few pennies. If the comfrey seems to be suffering from too much cutting by midsummer, it will perk up wonderfully when sprayed with liquid chicken manure. It pongs, too, but not nearly as badly as the comfrey.

Middy reminds me that there is a third excellent organic fertiliser, which is completely free. 'Pee,' she says holding up a bucket she is carrying to the tap. 'Dilute ten to one with water and it does wonders for my tomatoes. It is also good for getting the compost going.'

Pick more broad beans. Split a couple open and eat the beans out of the pods. Young and small like this, they are nutty and sweet and quite tender. Spray the growing tips of the plants with liquid detergent in water, trying to avoid the flowers and the pods further down. Kneel down to check the effect. As far as I can tell, the soapy water is just running over the massed bodies of blackfly, leaving them unaffected and dripping to the ground. Make up a solution of washing soda and spray the gooseberries, which have mildew again.

Friday
The weeds in the onion bed are so thick that they are hiding some of the onions and I am chopping them out with the hoe by mistake. I am going to have to do this the hard way, on my knees pulling the weeds up by hand or with the trowel. It is hot and clouded over and muggy, and as I am in shorts, I put on knee pads, mainly to stop the red ants from stinging me. Every half a row I fill a bucket which I take to the wooden compost bin. My shirt is soon soaked with sweat and it is running into my eyes. My back and shoulders ache and at least one ant has got around the pad and stung me on the leg inside the shorts. This is really hard work.

The second time I am stung I slap my leg with the trowel, which does me no good at all, and swear loudly. It takes me a few moments to realise that the remedy is to hand. Onions. This is a tip I read about in the medical-advice column of a paper and it does work. I retrieve one of the hoed onions, slice it in half and apply the cut surface to the sting. It starts to soothe the skin within a minute. It works for all stings, including nettles, as well as cuts and bruises. While I am wondering how to keep the onion in place so that I can carry on working, there is a flash of lightning followed almost immediately by an almighty crash of thunder. Fat drops of rain plop onto the earth. The sky has darkened alarmingly.

I struggle awkwardly to my feet, using the hoe as a prop. There is another flash of lightning which I swear goes over my head and hits the ground two allotments away. It is blinding and frightening. I throw the hoe down and sprint for the shed and once inside with the door shut start to worry that it is the highest structure in this area. The rain is coming down now like a tropical storm, beating on the roof and almost drowning out the rolls of thunder. A wind has got up from nowhere and is thrashing the beans and cabbages and whipping plastic bags and paper up into the air. I am almost too frightened to look out of the window, and when I do I see lightning hit the tower of St Jude's Church twice in quick succession. The rain is being driven under the roof felt and is dripping through in half a dozen places. I duck down to try to find a dry spot and knock over a four-pack of beer. I brought it down weeks ago intending to put it in jam jars to use as slug traps. My need is greater than theirs, and though it is warm, I gratefully open a can and drink while the storm crashes and flashes around my fragile little refuge.

Sunday

Pop down early morning to lift the first of the early potatoes for lunch. It is much cooler after the storm, and the Viola Cornetti French beans have curled up their purple-edged leaves like children wrapping their arms around themselves after dipping their toes into a chilly sea.

The rain has plumped up the potatoes. The first plant I fork up yields ten tubers and the second fifteen, together weighing about 3 pounds, which will be enough for today. The Ace Cultivator sees what I am doing and brings over a handful of the mint which grows wild beside his plot to add to the cooking water. There will be more than enough over to make fresh mint sauce for the roast lamb. Pick more sweet peas and raspberries, and a few sprigs of redcurrants, which have ripened early. Do some more weeding and by the time the church clock strikes noon, the clouds have cleared and it is hot again.

On the way home drop into the off licence beside the church for a bottle of wine to go with the lamb. The lady behind the counter exclaims with delight when she sees the sweet peas. I take a handful out of the bunch and give them to her and she insists on giving me the wine at half-price. The door tings and in bustles the Hon. Sec., unusually smart in crisp shirt and tie. He has been to church, and tells me that one of the lightning strikes the other day blew a stone pinnacle off the corner of the tower and it crashed into the churchyard.

'It's that big,' he says, indicating a good-sized marrow. 'Thank goodness there was no one underneath, because it would have killed them.'

By late afternoon it is raining again and thunder rumbles in the distance, but it doesn't come in this direction.

Monday
Saleem's sapling is in a bad way. The leaves have withered and are hanging down on dry stalks. With the pruning knife I scrape away a small surface area of bark. If it is green underneath, it is still alive. It's brown. The sapling is dead. I pull and it comes straight out of the ground. The roots never took hold. I chuck it on to the bonfire pile of uncompostable material. Oh, well, I'll try again in the autumn.

Another heavy session of hoeing and pulling weeds. The rain has got them popping up everywhere, and other things, too. Slugs and snails are under every plant, and when I lift the planks I use for walking on the beds so that my feet don't compress the soil, the undersides are encrusted with them. Woodlice, too, though I think they only eat decaying matter. Damage is widespread, and some of the slugs are a rusty orange and about 5 inches long. Quite disgusting to look at, and far too big for the greediest frog or magpie to eat. When I take the watering can over to the pumpkin and courgette plantlets, I find that they have all been eaten down to the stems. The Viola Cornetti French beans have been ravished. Bites have even been taken out of the stalks of rhubarb. Action is called for.

There are still two cans of beer in the shed and I fetch them together with a plastic bag of jam jars and yogurt pots. I bury these up to their rims among susceptible plants and pour an inch or two of beer into them. The slugs go in for a drink and can't get out again and drown. That's the theory, anyway. I'll see.

Tuesday
Three slugs, a snail, a couple of beetles and several woodlice. That is all I have caught with sixteen jars and pots. Slugs probably climbed in last night in their hundreds, drank the beer and climbed out roaring drunk and sang all the way home. I must find another way. Confucius might have some ideas.

There is no sign of him on his plot, but I follow the smell of exotic cigarette smoke to the shed and take the precaution of calling: 'It's only me.'

A furtive eye appears at the window. 'Be with you in a minute.' His plot ignores the usual allotment conventions of straight lines and neat beds, like Poppy's does, but lacks her flamboyant swirls of pattern and colour. He seems to like circular beds. Perhaps they are a New Age or hippie idea for channelling energy or something. In one there is – I go closer to make sure – a long-stemmed variety of oats or barley. Now that is something I have not seen before on an allotment. In another is buckwheat, which he has let go to flower. It looks rather like oilseed rape.

Two compost bins are full of rejects from the organic greengrocers and there seem to be three more bins under construction from pallets and assorted lumber. A sailing dinghy on a trailer is parked by the fence, and there are a lot of things which have been rescued from skips with an eye to making something useful out of them. A large gas cylinder and a cast-iron drainpipe are being put together to make a solid-fuel stove.

'Do you see the buckwheat?' he says when he joins me, picking shreds of tobacco out of his beard. 'It attracts lacewings and hoverflies which eat aphids by the million.'

'But why are you growing barley?' I ask.

'For the straw. I am going to use it to insulate the compost bins, where it will provide a habitat for lots of small creatures. Look here.' He shows me a tennis ball with a small hole cut in

the side which has been fastened to several wheat stalks. 'That
will make a nest for harvest mice.'

I grunt. 'Why attract mice?'

'They eat seeds and get eaten by foxes, man. It's all part of the
circle of life.'

'Right. That's what I've come to ask you about. I want something to eat my slugs.'

'Um. Frogs?'

'Got those. They're not up to it.'

'Ducks?'

'Too much trouble.'

'Hedgehogs?'

'Great. Where do I get them from?' He shakes his head. 'Have
you ever seen one round here? I haven't.' He shakes his head
again. I sigh. It's a pity that bumblebees don't eat slugs because
I seem to have more and more of them visiting my plot. What
now? I ring the R.H.S. advice line at Wisley and ask them. The
advisor admits he has a terrible slug problem, too, and has tried
everything without much success.

'In desperation,' he says, 'I go around the garden at night
with a torch spotting them crawling over plants.'

'Then what?' I ask.

'I cut them in half with secateurs.' He gives a demented
giggle. I know exactly how he feels.

Wednesday

Ali is telling me about his knack for discovering unusual and off-
beat things to grow simply by ferreting around on market stalls
and in supermarkets. It is amazing how well some exotic imports
adapt to an English allotment.

Last year he tried out passion fruit. This year it is South
African garlic and Dutch onions. He shows me the garlic with a
sense of theatre, leading me up a path, gesturing to me to stop
and go down on my knees, as he does, and then parting a curtain
of foliage to reveal it. I gasp. 'Wow!'

It is like a plantation of young palm trees, and at the base of

each one there is a red-skinned bulb nearly the size of a tennis ball. 'Is very, very good. And strong,' he says, kissing his finger-tips with lip-smacking relish. 'And here, look.' He scuttles off across the plot, past the shed which has a floor and a roof, a chair and a table, but no walls, to the onion bed. He pulls one and holds up a distinctive egg-shaped bulb.

'Not sharp. Sweet and crisp. On a bus yesterday I take one and peel. People give me funny look and stop talking. I smile.' He smiles a roguish smile like a cad in a Victorian melodrama.

'Then I bite it, like apple. People are shocked and the woman opposite me nudge her friend and say, "Look at that crazy for-eigner. He's eating a raw onion."' He laughs. He says he cut another onion into small pieces and passed it around the bus and persuaded people to try it, and the woman who said he was crazy loved it and asked for more.

Oh, foolish woman. Ali will be boarding your bus any day now with his charming, roguish smile and a big bunch of raw garlic which he will make you eat.

Thursday
I discover the bumblebees that are everywhere are not visitors but tenants. As I top up one of the old compost bins with stable

manure from the free tractorload that has been dumped by the gates, I notice one or two bees hovering between my legs and the side of the bin. I think they may be attracted by the manure. Each time I bring a new barrowload there are more and when there are half a dozen all hanging about in the same area, I realise something is wrong and back away. Do bumblebees swarm? I don't know. I still don't know if they sting or not.

Hurry over to find Confucius. He was planning to build a hive inside his shed so he must know something about bees. He's not there, and peering through the window I can see nothing that resembles a hive, though who knows with him. It could be in that kitchen dresser on the back wall, or the enormous 1940s radio.

Find the Birdman tending his dahlias and drag him away. There are about a dozen big black bumblebees buzzing around the bin when we get back and they are clearly agitated.

'Where did you first see them?' he asks. I pick up a bamboo cane and point. He takes the cane and clears away the fresh manure that has fallen from the barrow against the side of the bin, moving slowly to avoid alarming the bees. Magic and Saleem join us. Before he has finished one of the bees detaches itself from the squadron and flies on to a wooden cross bar that is now uncovered and crawls forward and disappears. Another follows.

'See what happened? You blocked the entrance to the nest and they couldn't work out how to get in. You'll be all right now,' he says, straightening up and handing me back the cane.

'All right? With a bees' nest there? They could sting me at any time.'

'Just leave them alone and they'll work around you.'

'Pfui,' snorts Saleem in disagreement.

Magic says, 'Bumblebees were nesting in the ground among my cabbages in the spring and I dug them out.' So that's where they came from. He adds meaningfully: 'You never know with bees.'

'That's right,' says Saleem. 'The main path here goes right by the entrance to the nest. You might annoy them without even knowing it, or the children might, and then they'll sting. Better kill them.'

But killing bees is monstrous, like telling a child Father Christmas does not exist. In an anguish of indecision I watch the bees coming and going all afternoon, bumbling gently about, the essence of fruitfulness and goodness in a garden. I know I will be constantly tense while the nest remains, shouting at the children every time they go near, and digging it out would be like trying to defuse a bomb without instructions.

I buy a can of insecticide and with a heavy heart spray the entrance and repeat every time I see a bee enter or leave. After a while none leave and a little while after that no more arrive. I feel as though I have violated nature.

Saturday
The slug damage is worse than ever. In the Hut Queeny gives me a cup of tea and a slice of Dundee cake with toasted almonds on top and says: 'Have you tried eggshells broken up small? They can't stand crawling over them.' I try to guess how many eggs I would need to make a barrier around my plants. A couple of hundred?

'You should have done what I did,' says Saleem. 'When the manure was delivered, instead of binning it you should have laid it out on the ground like a carpet. That way it suppresses the weeds and the slugs, keeps in moisture and the worms do the job of digging it in for you.' He laughs with delight at the neatness of his method, an all-in-one solution to a gardener's problems.

'Soot,' says Sailor. 'Slugs won't crawl over that because it gums them up.'

'You can't get it round here any more,' says Queeny.

Rita, who is helping out with Queeny, reaches up to the shelves for a selection of toxic chemicals and lays the packets out on the counter. The Polish family comes in and everyone turns to give them their attention. Their understanding of English is so limited that it takes mother, father, grandmother and grandad all working together to produce one understandable sentence. It is different when the children are with them because they went to school down the road and speak English as well as anyone here, but now they are teenagers they don't come much any more. The mother has the unenviable task of putting together their request, with many Polish words offered on her side and possible English meanings batted back from the rest. Mutual incomprehension follows.

I pick up a couple of the packets which bear lurid B-movie pictures of giant slugs and caterpillars and aphids taking over the world. 'I can't use these,' I say to Rita. 'I'm organic.'

The grandmother points at what I am holding and shrieks: '*Tak, tak!*' and the others nod vigorously and smile. So they have a bad slug problem too. I go looking for Middy, who will know what the organic treatment for slugs is, but she is not here today, so I push a note under the door of her shed explaining the problem.

The leaves on the garlic are still yellowish, though no worse than when I stopped watering them so they may be recovering. The shallot leaves have gone thoroughly yellow and dry-looking. There is nothing wrong with them. They have finished growing and need the soil drawn back from the clusters of bulbs to let the sun ripen them. Each shallot, planted months ago, has turned into a tight little bunch of eight or so bulbs. Where the leaves have fallen off they look like a clutch of brown eggs.

The red- and blackcurrants will be ready soon and I should net them to keep the birds off. They go for the red ones, which are more visible. The blackcurrants, carried under the leaves and out of sight, are fat and juicy, though still tart to the taste. I reckon some of them will be as big as grapes.

Monday
Poppy waves to me. She is wearing a wide straw hat with a flowery scarf looped around the crown and hanging down her back in two tails and looks as if she is off to a garden party. She has my note to Middy in her hand, and says: 'There is no organic way of controlling slugs which really works.' Just as I feared.

'But there is an organic way of killing them with slug pellets.' This sounds like the logic of Mad Alice. 'No, really,' she says, reading my expression accurately. 'It is approved by the Soil Association.' Ah, the Soil Association, governing council of the organic world. Should I bow at the mention of their name?

'What you do is this.' She picks up a square sectioned plastic water bottle, cuts a slit down the middle of one side with short cross cuts at each end to create two flaps, and bends these inwards. 'Put a spoonful of slug pellets inside with a stone or two to weight it down and put it where slugs are active. You can half bury it if you like, but the square section will stop it rolling over. Slugs and snails climb in, eat the pellets and die. The pellets and their chemicals don't go into the ground, nothing else can get at the pellets in there to eat them, and birds and hedgehogs can't eat the poisoned slugs and die themselves. What do you think?'

'A perfect closed system for killing slugs. Brilliant. Where do I get thirty square bottles?'

Wednesday
The allotments were burgled last night. It was done so neatly and with such discrimination and care that it must have been a professional job. I wonder if there is an Allotment Gang, well known in the underworld, which tours the country plundering allotment sites.

The thieves cut through the chain-link fence under the street light which has never worked and broke into forty sheds. They were looking for tools. They took so many that they used half a dozen wheelbarrows to cart off their loot and kept those as well, so they must have had a large van waiting.

They chose their targets by looking through shed windows, and where the windows were covered with opaque plastic, they cut neat flaps in it to see what was inside. They forced doors and on the Manager's shed, where the door was reinforced with steel panels and secured with three locks, they simply crowbarred the end wall off.

They were very cool customers, with plenty of time and no fear of being disturbed, because they sorted through drawers and boxes for hand tools and money and put everything else back. They took cans of beer but not cans of soft drink, proper wine but not home-made wine. They were considerate in comparison with what the vandals do. At least they did not set fire to the sheds and smash greenhouses, which is probably why people have taken this blow with resignation rather than rage.

The tools will be sold off within the next few days at car-boot sales. Has anyone worked out how much car-boot sales have contributed to an increase in crime by making it worthwhile for people to steal low-value goods which can be sold virtually without risk? Though not entirely risk-free: one allotmenteer who was robbed a while ago spotted his tools at a car-boot sale on a stall run by a fellow allotment holder and called the police.

The thieves ignored my shed, probably because the window was covered by fencing panels, which they couldn't be bothered to move to see if there was anything worth stealing.

Thursday
Carlo tells me that Poppy is working too hard on the allotment. She smiles brightly and says these long, hot days are so wonderful she can't keep away. 'You know it starts to get light at half past three in the morning. Sometimes I wake up then, when the birds start their dawn chorus, and I have to get up and come down here. I was down this morning before five and it was like another world, so calm and peaceful, as if it had been freshly made. The foxes were walking about as if they owned the place. You should try it.' She is so enthusiastic that I think 'Why not?', and back at home set the alarm for five.

Friday
When the alarm goes off I look at it in disbelief, having forgotten why I set it. The last time I was awake at this time was years ago, when I was single and party hopping. No, it was when the children were babies. My head drops back and hits the pillow. No,

don't go back to sleep. I struggle out of bed and dress and go downstairs still half-asleep. When I open the front door, it is more like January than June out there. Rain is bouncing off the path and the sky is so dark with cloud that the street lights are still on. If foxes are out in this weather, they deserve to have the allotments to themselves. I turn round and stumble back to bed.

Saturday
The first of the summer parties is a barbecue in the Hon. Sec.'s garden. The weather has cleared; it is warm and dry and the recent rain has brought out all the scents of the flowers and herbs. He is cooking boned legs of lamb over charcoal, served with new potatoes, sugar snap peas, stick beans and salad, and followed by soft fruit or rhubarb fool, all – apart from the meat – from the allotments. Oh, and his home-made wine, too.

There are about forty people, all dressed far more smartly than I have ever seen them before. There is a steady buzz of conversation about crops and how things are doing and who is up to what. The wine is surprisingly good considering it has been made from almost every fruit in the Hon. Sec.'s allotment, including currants, gooseberries, apples and grapes. By the third glass I feel very relaxed and comfortable, and as the moon comes up over the honeysuckle hedge at the bottom of the garden, I think how good it is to be among friends who have a common purpose.

July

Sunday

'What happened to you last night?' asks the Hon. Sec. He looks up from his task of planting leek seedlings into deep holes that he has made with a super dibber, the shaft and handle of a spade with the blade removed, but doesn't get up from his knees or stop work. His wife and two children are all working at different spots on the plot, which is immaculate. The beds are neatly edged with timber boards, the paths are closely mown and all his plant supports, from flower stakes to the arches carrying climbing roses and blackberries, are made from matching wooden stakes rather than the hodge-podge of bamboo, rusty iron pipes and discoloured plastic tubes which disfigure most plots.

'I had to rush home on an errand of mercy,' I reply. The boys rang to say they were playing in the garden at dusk with the dog when she jumped for a stick and missed, and the stick hit her in the eye and made it bleed.

'Is the dog all right?'

'Yes. I took her to the vet this morning and she said it was the eyelid, not the eye, luckily.' Dogs are not allowed on the allotments, even on leads. I always resented that until one evening when I took my normally well-behaved Labrador down anyway for company, thinking no one would be around to see her. She got so excited by all the new smells that she wriggled out of her collar and raced away across the plots in the dark doing goodness knows what on them. She came back after fifteen minutes covered in the smelly compost she had rolled in and eating something unmentionable. Then I understood.

'I wanted to say how much I enjoyed the barbie. The food was brilliant.'

'Good. We made a profit of nearly £200.' Tickets to the barbecues cost £6, slightly more for non-members of the Allotment Association, and the money left over after the food and drink are paid for funds other allotment activities, including the winter lectures in the church hall. Even after the lectures we are building up a healthy surplus, though not enough yet to meet the Hon. Sec's. ambitious plans to buy mechanical cultivators and shredders. Nor has he yet worked out where we will store them on our vandal-prone site, or who will maintain and clean them.

He stands up and briefly brushes down his electric-blue Bermuda shorts with a muddy hand before driving the spade handle into the ground in half a dozen places, making holes well over a foot deep and 2 inches in diameter. He takes leeklets from a tray and drops them into the bottom of the holes, sluicing in plenty of water so that their roots will be anchored in mud. The leeks will grow up towards the light and their stems will gradually fill the hole and be blanched white for the length of it. I suddenly wonder why. 'Why is that?'

'Hm?'

'Why are leeks grown underground, as it were, away from the light so that the stems are white? Does it give them a better flavour or texture, or what? I wonder what green leeks taste like? I have had green and white celery at the same time and I don't think I could taste any difference between them, and the same for asparagus.'

He sits back on his heels as if considering what I've said, but he hasn't heard me. 'I didn't get the chance to tell you last night about the allotments going on the Internet,' he says. 'We have a web page designed by Stu, our very own webmaster, and he's keen to get contributions from everyone.'

'Oh?' I hope I don't sound unimpressed; it's just that this news baffles me. I can't see any obvious connection between the electronic information revolution and the age-old activity of gardening, which still moves at a pre-Industrial Revolution pace and always will. For a moment I bizarrely wonder how he is going to arrange for people to connect to the Internet from their allotments, where we don't have telephone lines or even electricity. 'What's it for?'

'To spread the word about allotments, recruit new members, make contact with other allotment sites all over the country, share experiences and outings, guard against attempts by councils to sell sites off for development, try to raise funds from wherever we can, maybe even the Lottery . . .'. He goes on with e-vangelical zeal until my head spins with all the e-laborate wonders that he parades before me. 'We have to keep up with the times, you know,' he concludes, as if he suspects me of being hopelessly backward. 'Here.' He takes a pencil out of his pocket and writes on the back of a seed label: www.allotments.org. 'That's the address. Have a look when you get home.'

I do, and am very impressed at how professional and interesting it is. Among the many photographs is a panoramic view of the allotments on a bright day in early spring, looking towards the west and the tower of St Jude's Church. It has been taken from the Ridgeway and in the left foreground is my allotment, edged by the new trellis and neat and tidy, not weedy and ragged as it is now. There is also a ground plan of the site and a click on an allotment rectangle brings up a photograph of it and its tenant together with a little story about how he or she came to take it on and what they grow. In half an hour I learn more about some of my neighbours than I previously found out over several years.

Tuesday

Discover where Father Christmas goes in the summer: to Magic's allotment to scare the birds. Magic has realised that the starlings have got the polystyrene cat figured out for a couch potato and has replaced it with a Father Christmas figure, looking rather hot in his floppy red hat. He is also wearing an expression of puzzled surprise, as if he can't work out why he is here and not in Lapland with his feet up by the fire. A puff of wind makes him turn creakily round to survey the gooseberries. From this angle he looks rather sad, as if wondering where his reindeer have gone. Still, he must have the starlings seriously worried. There is not one in the cherry tree.

Thursday

The Ace Cultivator gives me four cucumbers, the short, rough-skinned type which look like overgrown gherkins. He advises me to keep them in the fridge to stop them tasting bitter. I have never grown cucumbers, mainly for lack of a greenhouse, but also because a few of them go a long way and they don't keep. I have never grown aubergines either, for the same reason, though I see Ace has several plants growing happily outdoors carrying egg-sized purple fruit, so perhaps I should try those next year.

The onions need weeding again. Where do all these weeds come from? Make sure I'm wearing knee pads to stop the ants from stinging me when I kneel down.

Friday

Set about lifting the garlic with some trepidation. It has a reputation for being virtually problem-free and of more or less
growing itself. Certainly it will grow happily in most soils, so
long as it gets plenty of sun, and it needs no special treatment.
But as I found last month after Saleem ticked me off, it is prone
to rot if it gets too wet at the wrong time. I keep forgetting when
I have the hose out to give the plot a drenching that garlic orig-
inates from hotter and drier climates and it does not need much
water.

I have grown it in two beds and my fears are confirmed when
I fork up the first. Many of the bulbs are slimy and they have lost
part of their protective outer papery membrane. They are also
small. They may still be usable but they don't look right and they
won't keep long, a few weeks only.

'Oh, dear,' says Rita from across the fence. 'Ours weren't
good either, and Chicken Tom pulled up all his and burned
them. I blame the weather in the spring.'

'They're not all bad,' I say. 'We'll just have to cook everything
in garlic before they go off.'

'You could bottle them and cover with salted water. They'll
keep like that in the fridge for quite a while. Or do what I do and
chop them and freeze on a tray so they stay loose, then pack into
yogurt pots with lemon juice in the freezer and just take out a
spoonful when you're cooking.'

The story is completely different when I go to the other bed.
The bulbs are as perfect as I could hope, fat and round and
enveloped in a membrane which is white with purple markings
like the ones which come from the south of France, but bigger.

The seed was the same for both, so what happened? The
first bed was covered with a layer of wood chips a couple of
inches thick to suppress weeds. This also kept the soil permanently moist, so the garlic rotted. The second bed was left
uncovered and dried out easily. The lesson could not be clearer:
garlic hates being damp. I shall listen more carefully to Saleem
in future.

Take them home to dry and ripen on the garden table, and then to string up after selecting the best for the show. Feel certain these bulbs are going to win me a first prize.

Garlic is about the only kitchen plant which Arthur ignores, reflecting an almost universal aversion to the taste of it by his and my parents' generations of English people. To them it symbolised the decadence and sinfulness of Continental life. On trips to France my mother always caused embarrassment to the family and bemusement to waiters by insisting in every restaurant that her food should be cooked without garlic. I can almost sense Arthur standing beside me now, sniffing disdainfully at what I consider to be the beautiful aroma of garlic rising from the table.

Monday

Have a shock when I open the door of the shed. Bindweed is creeping through the planks of the back wall and pushing up through gaps in the floorboards. Not just one or two tentative shoots, but a dozen determined runners. It has wrapped itself around the handles of the rake and the draw hoe, perhaps knowing they aren't used much at the moment, and is twirling up them. Go outside to uproot the plants and discover that the old raspberry bed is full of the stuff.

There is no organic way of treating bindweed, and my non-organic friends say the strongest sprays in their chemical arsenal only check it for a week or two before it grows back. The only answer is to get hold of the plants at ground level and try to pull up as much root as I can. They go down so deeply that it is impossible to dig all the roots out, and trying to do so here would cause havoc with the raspberries. This is a thankless, sweaty job on a hot day, inching through the plantation on my hands and knees and getting scratched all over my arms and legs by the spines on the raspberry canes and being buzzed at by wasps. An hour and a half's work produces a big pile of weeds and an awful lot of healthy raspberry canes with masses of immature fruit accidentally yanked out in my impatience, which puts me in a foul temper.

Go and kick the bale of straw which makes me feel better. Bits of straw fly everywhere, but no matter. Sit down on the battered bale and reflect that what I should do to induce an atmosphere of calm is make a set of wind chimes out of the tubular steel sections of the children's old climbing frame lying under one of the blackthorn bushes. It would be a huge set because the tubes range from 2 to 6 feet in length, but then wouldn't it be hugely calming? Or maybe hugely clamorous.

Open the Tardis for the first time for weeks half expecting to see a horde of mice. There is no sign of them and the multi-coloured mish-mash of peelings, leftovers, sweepings, newspapers and egg cartons has turned a uniform chocolate brown. Lower my head and sniff tentatively. It smells earthy and good. Get the fork and poke about. It looks good all the way down, and it is riddled with worms, the thin red ones known as tiger worms, which feed exclusively on decaying organic matter. I don't know where they came from but there must be hundreds of them, which is excellent as they make compost so good that it can be used for growing seeds and is excellent for perking up tired pot plants. Nature has performed the mysterious alchemy of turning garbage into brown gold. I fork it all out and use it to top dress the beans, raspberries, corn and blackberries.

The sweet peas are covering the trellis in blooms, and I cut a bunch so big that I need two hands to hold it and still drop flowers all the way to the gate. Exit stage left pursued by bees.

Tuesday
The runner beans have reached the top of the poles, 7 feet up, and are still trying to climb, fuelled by trenchfuls of compost. I move along the dense green hedge pinching off the tips to stop them twining back on themselves and growing into knots, and try to avoid disturbing the bees on the clusters of scarlet flowers. They are growing much more lushly than the French beans beside them. The rows are too close together and although I thought I compensated for that with the compost and the liquid feed of chicken manure I give them at least once a week, the

Viola Cornettis don't like being crowded. Or maybe they don't like being in the shadow of the runners when the sun goes behind them in the afternoons.

It is hot again and it is tempting to linger in the cool shade between the beans. The murmur of the bees is a lullaby which makes me feel sleepy, and the air is heavy with the scent of flowers and earthiness. I'll just sit down for two minutes. The soil is warm and cushioned with dry compost, and it pillows my shoulders and head. Mmm, bliss.

I close my eyes for what I think is about half a minute, but when I open them again the shadows have lengthened and my watch shows that I have been asleep for nearly an hour. I have never done that before – fallen asleep on the ground in the day – and it feels delightfully decadent and self-indulgent. For a while longer I lie there gazing up into the deep blue of the sky and listening to the muted sounds of birdsong and people working. I rouse myself finally when I feel a beetle wriggling inside my shirt.

Wednesday
The autumn-sown onions are ready to lift. Their leaves died down last month and I left them in place to dry off and ripen. Now, when I come to lift them with the fork, I find they are much smaller than I expected. I planted them as sets in October and after nine months in the ground, most of them are not much bigger than golf balls. They are supposed to fill the gap when the previous year's stored main-crop onions have run out and this year's main crop are not yet ready. But the main onions which were planted in February are already much bigger than these and I could be pulling some of those now if I needed them.

I can hold half a dozen bulbs in one outstretched hand. This is very disappointing. It is not worth growing them and tying up a bed for most of the year if this is all I am going to get at the end of it.

Cheer myself up by lifting four Charlotte potato plants, half filling a carrier bag with the plump oval tubers. They are the best summer potato I have ever grown for taste and texture and will be my regular choice from now on. Also lift one of the Pink Fir Apples to see how they are doing. The nobbly tubers are only a couple of inches long and quite narrow, which is not surprising as they are a main crop which should be left in the ground until September. By then they will have grown three times as big and each of the nobbles will be as large as the main tuber is now. They are impossible to peel or scrape, which doesn't matter as they are so good cooked with the skins on as a salad potato or added to any meal. Their firm flesh is waxy with a nutty flavour. I will lift them weekly from now on, not too many at a time but enough so there are leftovers. I raid the fridge for these and, when no one else is looking, dip the cold P.F.A.s into gravy or houmous, or spread a little bit of Stilton cheese on them. Piggy, but yummy.

Pick about a pound and a half of French beans. There are some on the inside of the frame behind leaves, where I have missed them before, which are at least 6 inches long. They are still slimmer than a pencil and will be stringless and perfectly good to eat. They don't coarsen until the pods become 'beany' later in the season.

Gather peas and eat some of them straight out of the pod after checking for weevils, which are bad this year. Cut lots of courgettes. When they are small like this, not much more than the length of a finger, I split them lengthwise and fry them in butter with finely chopped shallots and garlic and lots of black pepper. I have been meaning for years to try a recipe for courgette or marrow flowers which involves dipping the large, yellow trumpet-shaped blooms in batter and cooking in deep oil. When it comes to it I always duck out, fearing that if I cut enough flowers to make a worthwhile portion or two, I will be depriving myself of an awful lot of courgettes.

Pick spring onions, which are on the small side, lettuces, which are thickening a bit at the top as if they are threatening to bolt, and radishes. After briefly inspecting these I throw the lot on the compost. They have been left in the ground too long and gone thick and woody. It happens much more quickly at this time of year than in the spring. They also have patches chewed off by slugs, which is off-putting. Get a seed packet from the shed and sow more.

Thursday

The rhubarb is getting past it. The stems are thick and remain fibrous when cooked. It is like putting a spoonful of custardy string into the mouth. The plants have been mauled again by slugs or snails. They take small bites out of the stems which don't do any serious damage but do disfigure them so that they become even more unappetising.

Rhubarb would seem to be one of the least likely of plants to attract the creepy-crawlies, but they do. In my non-organic days I once put a ring of slug pellets round a crown of rhubarb and a few weeks later I counted seventy-four snail shells. Boiled rhubarb leaves were once used by gardeners to control pests, though now do-it-yourself pesticides are frowned on, and in some cases actually illegal. Rhubarb leaves are highly poisonous to humans, so I would not want to boil them up in my kitchen anyway. Stewed rhubarb should never be mixed with pineapple because they produce an acidic chemical reaction which can be dangerous if eaten.

The gooseberries are finishing, too, and I have a momentary pang of fruit deprivation and wish that I was still growing strawberries. Though when I did, I found them more trouble than they were worth. The bed became infested with couch grass, which couldn't be dug out, and I always lost more than half the crop to slugs, mould and birds.

Chide myself that I really have no reason to feel deprived. The raspberries are producing a bumper crop, the greengages are luscious and the small crop of peaches will be ready any day now, not to mention the blackberries.

The tomato plants are growing vigorously, and the main stalks need to be tied to the supporting bamboo canes and the side shoots pinched out. If left, they pop out everywhere, diverting the plant's energy into leafy growth, and the tomatoes they produce will be undersized. Actually, all the tomatoes look undersized and retarded. Feed with comfrey juice at the rate of a quarter of a pint to 2 gallons of water, which I pour into the pots and plastic bottles set into the ground by the plants.

A good side effect of this technique is that it stops me from watering on to the soil around the plants and splashing them. This is one of the ways in which blight is passed rapidly from plant to plant.

On the way home, pass the Ace Cultivator's plot and see that some of his tomatoes are carrying trusses of such huge fruit that he has had to rig up slings to support them and stop them tearing their branches off. I interrupt his raspberry picking to ask what his secret ingredient is. He smiles in an apologetic way.

'None.'

'But they look ten times as big as mine, and nearly ripe, too.' My Inner Saxon Peasant gives an edge of disappointment to my voice.

'I did start them off early in the conservatory at home, and I feed them a lot. The variety, Shirley, is a heavy cropper.' He gives me a handful of raspberries as a consolation prize.

Friday

The pigeons have been at the cabbages which Rita gave me. The outer leaves on three of them have been eaten down to the ribs, giving them a skeletal appearance. The damage is bad and on any other plant it would probably be fatal. However, cabbages are very resilient and they will recover quickly with plenty of watering.

I've brought a tape player with an assortment of tapes filched from around the house. I reckon the tomatoes need a little music to put them in the mood for growing. What would they like? My boys are both into heavy metal, grunge, jungle, drum and bass. Mmm, not very suitable.

I know. Think tomatoes, think Italy, think opera. How about this: *The Marriage of Figaro*. I leave it playing among the plants for an hour while I weed and water. Whenever I straighten up and look around, I intercept curious glances from one distant plot holder after another. I just smile and nod and drop down out of sight.

The sweetcorn is a bit backward. Perhaps that would perk up with music, too. The choice here is more difficult. When I think of sweetcorn I think of the American west. Indian country. But I think it was first cultivated in South America, so what I need is Andean pan pipes, or the Tijuana brass. I'm out of luck. The closest I have is Eric Clapton. Eric Clapton? It's that or the Rolling Stones.

'What are you doing?' asks Saleem, appearing around the end of the beans. He laughs when I explain and I switch the tape off in embarrassment. He points to one of the tomato plants which has broken free of its ties and is sprawling across the ground. 'You would be better off layering that one, and any others which can't support themselves.' I have never heard of layering tomatoes, or any annual plant, apart from sweet peas. He shows me.

Where the stem touches the ground – in two places in this case – he buries it, and makes sure the growing tip is clear and pointing upwards so that sap will continue to flow to it. 'At each of these points roots will form and new plants will grow which will be much sturdier than the parent because they will be fed by the main root as well as their own.'

When he goes, I put the Stones on again with the sound lowered. What will the sweetcorn make of 'Jumping Jack Flash'?

Lift more Charlottes because I gave so many from the last lifting away to friends and relatives, telling them to taste for themselves the difference between the chemically sprayed shop-bought ones and organic. Just showing off, really. Astonished to see that one of the tubers has a root of couch grass growing straight through it. The white root, as thick as a matchstick, has gone in one side and out the other as if it is a steel meat skewer. The tip is pointed and sharp when I touch it. The potato seems none the worse for the experience. I take it home and clean and cook it and it tastes fine.

Saturday

Is it my imagination or is the sweetcorn looking oddly dishevelled, with rumpled leaves? Rummage around in the tape bag for something calmer and less vocal than the Rolling Stones. John Williams playing Spanish dances on guitar. That should do. Go down to the Trading Hut for a roll of soft green twine and to cadge a cup of tea and catch up with the gossip. I shouldn't, because I have been so lazy recently – taking an afternoon nap between the beans is becoming a habit – that everywhere I look there are things which need doing.

Slipping out on to the path from behind the trellis I catch Alan talking to one of his apple trees and fail to suppress a smile of fellow feeling. From the way he gives a guilty start when he sees me, I suspect he misinterprets it as a mocking smile, so I tell him about the tapes.

'I wasn't talking to it,' he says. 'Not really. I was threatening to chop the bugger down with an axe unless it produces some apples.'

'Oh.'

'When I planted this one ten years ago, I planted another of the same sort in my garden and that gives lovely apples, which start off as cookers and with keeping become sweet enough to eat – I can't remember the name. This one never produces anything worth anything. So I've told it. "It's apples or you're firewood."'

'That's telling it, all right, even if you're not talking to it,' I say slyly. He smiles sheepishly.

Queeny is not running the Hut today. It's Rita, with Saleem and Sailor sitting to one side reading out titbits from their papers to each other. Manage to beg a cup of tea and a ginger biscuit off her. Tell them about the bindweed and as Saleem starts to say the only way of killing bindweed is to keep dipping the growing points in a jar of glyphosate, Brutally Frank interrupts him.

'I'll tell you a story about bindweed,' he growls. 'When they widened the railway out there to take another track fifty years ago, they had to dig a new cutting along towards the station. My dad was a railwayman and he had one of these allotments then and he took me down there to see something before they built the retaining wall.

'The cutting was vertical, like they'd taken a knife and sliced a cake, and he showed me roots of one bindweed plant going down 25 feet through the ground.' He stops talking and looks at us truculently as if we might doubt him. 'We measured it. Twenty-five feet down and 25 feet across, like a ruddy tree upside down. All that root and only 3 or 4 feet of the plant showing above ground. You can't dig that out, and you can spray and dip it as much as you like, but, to be brutally frank, nothing is going to kill it. As my dad said, you might manage to stop a few tendrils, but with all that underground power it will just keep throwing up more wherever it wants. You've just got to learn to live with it.'

Mad Alice comes in, followed by Poppy at a discreet distance and averting her nose. Despite the hot weather, Alice is as usual wearing a man's dirty raincoat tied around her middle with a clothes line, which has several pegs attached to it. She uses these to clip notes on to sticks beside plants reminding her of things which need doing. She asks for a pint of seaweed extract and Saleem gets up to decant this from a large drum into an empty whisky bottle.

'Some fool's playing a guitar up the hill,' she says. 'Is it Five Pints? I thought he played a trombone.'

'Saxophone,' corrects Sailor.

'What's the difference? It's all a racket.'

'Oh, that's me,' I say. 'I must have left the tape playing to encourage the plants.' I'm conscious of everyone turning to look at me. 'Sorry.' My voice trails off into an embarrassed silence.

Alice lifts her bottle by the neck as if it's an action she's accustomed to. 'Encourage the plants?' she says with withering scorn, heading for the door. 'Someone round here's mad and it's not me.'

As the door bangs behind her people start to giggle, and Brutally Frank says: 'That's what she thinks.'

124

Poppy murmurs to me: 'Well, I think your plants will be very encouraged. The guitar music is lovely.' Then she asks Rita for cabbage seed.

'You know you have to sow those with a 7-pound hammer, don't you?' says Sailor. Poppy is mystified. 'Cabbages must be grown in ground that is hard. If it's not, you must bang it down to compact it, otherwise the cabbages will run to seed before they heart up.'

'But I don't have a hammer.'

'The back of a spade will do. Or you could walk up and down the row for half an hour.'

I leave the Hut with her and outside she invites me to join her and Carlo and a few others for a barbecue on their plot later on. 'It's nothing special,' she says. 'Just a few sausages and whatever is growing that takes your fancy. But bring a bottle.'

While helping with the weekly shopping in Waitrose in the afternoon, I stop by the fruit counter which is displaying raspberries in tiny punnets of about a quarter of a pound each. I do a mental calculation and, astonished, call my wife over. 'Do you realise how much they are charging for those? About £6.50 a pound, and they are not even organic like mine.' I do a rapid circuit of the store and discover that these raspberries are more expensive, weight for weight, than lobster, salmon fillets and sirloin steak. I do another calculation, of how much I would make if I covered my plot with raspberry canes and sold the fruit to a supermarket. It works out at . . .

'How much do you think?' I ask everyone sitting around the barbecue later. There are various guesses, none of which even comes close. 'A few thousand pounds.' There are exclamations of surprise but no one is stimulated by the prospect of such riches to go commercial – in fact, if anything, the opposite.

'But would you want to do that?' asks Carlo, opening another bottle of wine.

'He couldn't. You're not allowed to,' says Middy, sounding rather alarmed.

'Traitor,' mutters Confucius.

Magic says, 'One plot wouldn't be enough. You'd get another and another and before you knew it you'd be a farmer with all their hassles, like getting up at five in the morning and filling in forms.'

'Where's the fun in growing for a supermarket?' says Poppy. 'This is where the fun is. Growing what you want, how you want, and eating it when you want.'

I look around the group and nod. Shadows are creeping over the plot and the sky is turning purple, edged with salmon pink behind the church tower where the sun is setting. I can smell honeysuckle and night-scented stock, and the rosemary and thyme that were thrown on to the barbecue give a Mediterranean flavour to the warm air. I hold out my glass to Carlo and he refills it. 'You're right,' I sigh with contentment. 'Of course you are.'

Sunday

The church bells are ringing out for morning service, annoying the pigeons that are circling the tower high up. I start picking over the old raspberry canes alongside the Ridgeway. I put these in about seven years ago and was going to lift and burn them last year because the crop was so poor, the berries small, dry and pippy, that I thought they must be exhausted. Magic said they probably just needed feeding up, so, as I could never find the time to do a proper job of digging them out and reconditioning the soil, I top dressed the canes with bone meal and a thick layer of compost soaked in liquefied chicken pellets and left them. It obviously did the trick because they are bearing very well now, and the new canes coming up for next year's crop are taller and more vigorous than the current ones.

Although I have already gathered lots of raspberries over the past few weeks, I succeed in filling two ice-cream cartons, leaving many unripe berries to come on. When I stiffly straighten up at the end of the row, I startle two blackbirds which fly out of the nearby blackcurrant bushes with loud screeches of protest. Put down the cartons to investigate the bushes, which means going down almost to soil level and peering up under the dense cloak of leaves which hide the currants from casual view.

The bushes are festooned with long clusters of currants. Some of the clusters are so heavy the branches are bending under their weight. I can tell they are ripe by the shininess of the skins. In fact, they are overripe – the ground under the bushes is speckled with fallen currants. More drop as I move branches to look. I'd better start picking straight away or I will lose them. Luckily, I always keep plenty of plastic bags in the shed.

At home I weigh the raspberries. Five pounds. More than £30 worth at supermarket prices. At lunch the family eats half of them, smothered in cream and ice cream, with hedonistic delight. A long time afterwards, when I can lever myself out of the chair, I set about turning the blackcurrants into jam.

Blackcurrant Jam
I don't wash the currants, as they have never been touched by anything other than rain and my fingers, just remove stalks and leaves. Measure into a large pan with an equal amount of sugar, a little bit of water and some lemon juice and boil until they reach setting point, which is when they become jam, about fifteen to twenty minutes. Ladle into warm jars, cover with screw-on lids and allow to cool before labelling and putting away.

The 10 pounds of currants plus sugar fill just twelve and a half jars. They are so thick with currants that they are more like jars of preserved fruit than jam. The boys come into the kitchen and fight to lick the spoons and plates used to test the jam for setting, so I know this is going to be a good batch, maybe worth entering for the show.

Thursday
It has been raining on and off for three days, quite heavily at times. On a quick visit to the plot rediscover an old loganberry on the southern boundary which I tried to rejuvenate last year by layering a stem. It has grown a new plant all right, and it has

fruited. But the extraordinary thing is that the fruit is a rasp-berry, not a loganberry, and a hard, sour one, too.

'Am I right in thinking,' I ask the Ace Cultivator, 'that logan-berries are hybrids of raspberries and blackberries?'

He strokes his chin while studying the plant. 'Well, yes, I think so. Like boysenberries and tayberries – which incidentally are very good. You must try the one I planted last year.'

'In that case they wouldn't breed true from seed or from cut-tings, would they? This one has reverted to the parent raspberry, and a pretty nasty one it must have been.'

'I think you must be right. Well, that's something I haven't come across before.'

Saturday

The summer social tonight is hosted by Stu and his wife. They have provided a lavish spread of Mediterranean food, served up in their garden backing on to the allotments. Greek music drifts out through the kitchen windows. The garden is delightful: small, but like a maze, with hidden paths and changing vistas and secret ponds and leafy alcoves.

As the clatter of knives and forks on plates subsides, Stu steps forward and raises a hand for our attention. 'Before everyone relaxes too much I have an announcement to make. As many of you will know, the council runs a Borough in Bloom competition every year. As well as the usual categories for gardens and parks and the hanging baskets outside pubs and shops, there is one for best allotment. Three of our plots were commended by the judges, which was very good.' A few claps break out, but Stu waves his hand for silence. 'But best of all, they awarded first prize to our Honorary Secretary and his wife here.' The clapping is wild, and the Hon. Sec., in a pair of candy-striped Bermuda shorts, stands and takes a bow, then urges his shyer wife to her feet to share the moment of triumph.

August

Sunday

A stack of entry forms for next month's flower and vegetable show has appeared in the Trading Hut, and at the sight of them I get a tremor of nervous excitement. Pick one up and hurry off to my plot to examine it in private. Get the folding chair out of the shed and sit down in the shade of the vine climbing over the roof where I hope not to be disturbed.

The word 'form' does not do it justice. It is a twelve-page booklet listing the classes, 115 of them, arranged in eight sections for vegetables, fruit, domestic or prepared foods, and various types of flowers, then setting out the rules and the scoring system, and ending with a page of Hints to Exhibitors.

The rules are brief, to the point and clearly written, so as to avoid ambiguity. I expect they are based on the Royal Horticultural Society's guides to exhibiting and have been honed over many years to avoid acrimonious disputes, which is why they state what may seem to be obvious, as in Rule 6: 'Only the exact number and kind of article quoted in the classes may be staged', in case anyone is tempted to slip a couple of fancy tarts from Class 69 into Class 70, 'Six plain scones'.

Not only is the judges' decision final, as stated in Rule 17, but to underscore it, Rule 18 warns: 'The Committee shall have the power to deal with any matter not otherwise provided for in these rules.'

The Hints read like a supplement to the rules: beer must be exhibited in plain brown 1-pint bottles; fruit must not be polished; damaged flowers must be removed. They unbend a little when it comes to vegetables. These should be cleaned, trimmed and arranged attractively, and 'Sheer size for the sake of size is unimportant compared to uniformity in size and colour. A good general yardstick in most classes is the size you would expect to find in the average family kitchen.'

That's encouraging, but I have a nagging feeling that something is missing, that the Hints are not giving the full story. The feeling is something to do with what happened last year, but I can't properly remember. When the judge disqualified my sloe gin in the red-wine class for being too strong – and not actually wine, anyway – I threw a wobbly and my memories of the rest of the show are vague and misty, which I'm sure was nothing to do with my insistence on drinking a generous amount of the gin to show that there was nothing wrong with it.

Ernie, the steward who accompanied the judge on his rounds, said to me after breaking the news of my disqualification: 'He was sipping elderberry and plum and damson wines and when he came to yours and tasted it, his head snapped back and his eyes popped.' He grinned and winked at me. 'I bet it's good stuff, eh? What about a tasting?' He already had a glass in his hand and was nodding his head eagerly, so I filled it up but took the glass and drank it myself. I was almost popping with indignation at the time.

The Hon. Sec. won every first prize in the wine and beer classes that year, and I vowed to make a comeback and challenge his monopoly. As it happened, I had made two batches of elderflower wine from blossom gathered from allotment hedges that May. I made it for my own use, without a thought of showing it, after coming across my father's old recipe. He also used to make a truly excellent apple wine, so I decided to make some of that last October as well.

Apple Wine

Fill a 2-gallon food-grade plastic bucket with coarsely chopped apples. Don't peel or core them – it takes too long. Dissolve 5 pounds of sugar in 3 or 4 pints of boiling water and pour over the apples. Add enough extra water to cover them. When cool, add wine yeast that has already been started. Cover bucket with lid or clean cloth and allow to ferment for two to three weeks, then strain liquid off pulp into glass flagons fitted with airlocks and allow to ferment out, which could take several months.

The flagons of apple juice fermented out months ago and were put into a cupboard alongside the elderflower to mature. It is time to inspect them again.

My reverie is shattered by an explosion of birds from Magic's cherry tree behind me. It is covered in a net but with so many large holes that Father Christmas could drive his sledge through it. There must be nearly a hundred starlings whooshing into the air as if all the cats of hell are after them, and the shock of their sudden eruption brings me to my feet.

A moment later Magic appears on the other side of the tree waving one arm and carrying a plastic bread crate under the other and puffing from the effort of trying to run up from the gate. He is followed by his wife, also carrying a bread crate and out of breath, and two daughters. They only appear once or twice a year, so this must be an important occasion. All of them are dressed extremely smartly, Magic in a dark suit, tie and hat, and the womenfolk in colourful summer dresses and high-heeled shoes, which are causing them problems as they keep sinking into the ground and threatening to trip them up. Mrs Magic also has a hat, a broad-brimmed confection of artificial flowers which she is clutching to her head with her free hand to stop it falling off.

They reach the tree and stand around it, getting their breath back. I call to him: 'Are you all right?'

He puts a hand on his chest as if to calm his heart. 'Yes . . . in a minute . . . thanks . . .'. When he can speak properly he says: 'I didn't think the cherries would be ready for a few days yet, but I had a phone call from Poppy to say the starlings were stripping the tree, so we've rushed straight down from church.' I feel I should have scared them away for him, but I was so engrossed in thoughts of the show that I hadn't even noticed they were there. Magic organises his family to pick the cherries, sending the daughters up a rickety home-made ladder into the tree amid many giggles which turn into shrieks and arguments.

Watch for a few minutes, but I am holding my breath in anticipation of one or both of them falling out of the tree and breaking legs and arms, so force myself to turn away and get on with some work. Start to water the plot – it hasn't rained for a while and the ground is very dry – but my attention is still being drawn by the shrieks, so I put the hose down and go for a walk-about to see what everyone is up to. There's only a trickle coming out of the hose, anyway.

This is one of my favourite activities: wandering around the site to see how other plots are doing and chatting to their tenants. I gather more useful advice this way than I get from any number of books and television gardening programmes, because other people are encountering the same problems under the same conditions as I am. The place is full today, though people are taking the opportunity to relax in the sun rather than do any serious work, and the walkabout takes a couple of hours.

When I get back the girls are safely down from the tree and picking leaves and twigs out of each other's clothes, and the two bread crates are piled high with pink cherries. 'How much do you think you've got?' I ask Magic.

'About 60 pounds,' he says. 'I reckon the birds got another twenty or thirty, but it could have been worse. By tomorrow there wouldn't have been a cherry left. Not bad when you remember how much we lost in the frost.'

'No help from Father Christmas, then?'

He laughs. 'No. The stupid birds have no idea who he is.'

Mrs Magic insists on giving me several pounds of cherries, and I quickly pick a bagful of French beans to give her in return.

Monday

Go down early to get the hose out before the sun is hot enough to scorch wet plants. Everywhere I went on my walkabout yesterday I heard the same anxiety about lack of water. It is not yet a drought; the wet winter and spring topped up the reservoirs, so there is unlikely to be a restriction on the use of hosepipes, but even a few weeks without rain at this time of year turns the place into a dustbowl. The surface soil varies over the site from light and sandy, like my plot, to stiff clay, though it all sits on a deep bed of gravel which begins a few feet down. It is what is called free draining, in other words, water goes straight through as if it is a colander. Once the relatively thin soil layer dries out we are in trouble, for no amount of hand watering can ever replenish it. The best one can do is keep the most vulnerable plants going.

In winter, when I don't need to water, I could stand in the middle of the plot holding the hose and the high pressure in the pipe will send a jet to the furthest corner and beyond. I could even stand there and water Saleem's dahlias by directing the jet over the top of his ramshackle greenhouse.

In the summer pressure is always low, and today water just wells out of the nozzle and dribbles to the ground. There is no hope of it reaching the beans, so I stick the hose into the watering can and ferry water over. Many plants will cope for a while in dry conditions, but not beans. They produce a huge amount of leaves, which constantly lose moisture through transpiration, like sweating, and it has to be replaced. If it isn't, they quickly stop producing beans and it is quite difficult to get them started again, even if water becomes plentiful.

After a while give up on the hose because it takes so long to fill the can, and take the can to the tank and dunk it there. Spend a couple of hours on the runner and French beans, then the tomatoes, sweetcorn, raspberries and salads, and back to the beans again. It is hard work, and I stop when the sun gets high and flop down in the shade between the beans with aching arms and shoulders.

Try to put the tape player on and find it is jammed. Fiddle with it and dislodge a squashed caterpillar, but it still won't play. I don't suppose the tomatoes or the sweetcorn need any encouragement to grow in this weather.

Wednesday

Heat lies over the allotments like a weight, pressing the energy out of people, plants and the soil itself. Everything droops listlessly. The trouble with having a taste of a Mediterranean climate in the middle of England is that there is no Mediterranean to jump into to cool down. Now, if I had extended the frog pond as I planned, I could at least have paddled in that.

It is too hot to work, and even thinking about it tires me out, so I strip down to my shorts and lie on the sunbed with my eyes shut and pretend that I am beside the Med. It works well until the Birdman comes by foraging for chickweed for his canaries. He cracks a joke about my pale legs, then compliments me on the French beans, which are thriving in the heat. He has never seen the purple-podded variety before, so I pick some for him.

'Mine have been useless,' he says. 'I sowed three lots. If I had a friend in Australia, I'd ring him up to see if they've come through down there because they sure as blazes haven't come through up here. It's the same with the beetroot. It's lack of water. That's global warming for you, and it will only get worse.'

He sounds unusually tetchy and irritable and I ask him why. 'I can't stand this weather, nor can my birds. It's far too hot. Give me some cloud and a drop of rain any day.'

'Why don't you take some clothes off? You'll feel cooler.' Like Saleem, he makes no concession to hot weather and is wearing thick trousers, a long-sleeved shirt buttoned up at the wrists and neck and a waistcoat.

'And get skin cancer? No fear. I tell you, if this is how the weather's going to be from now on then whenever I plant anything which is going to stay in the ground for more than a year I'm going to dig a deep trench first and fill it with as much compost as I can get hold of mixed with newspaper and rags and anything else which will hold moisture. I'll look in skips for old eiderdowns and duvets. Feather pillows would be good, and if I find one of those old-fashioned horsehair mattresses it would be perfect. That would keep something like an asparagus bed going for ten years.'

He sees the show form on the sunbed and asks what I will be entering. I shrug, not wanting to commit myself. 'It depends on what this weather does to things. And you?'

'Nothing, probably. I've had a terrible year.' He speaks loudly, then winks at me and taps the side of his nose. He drops his voice to a hoarse whisper. 'That's in case anyone is listening.' He nods meaningfully in the direction of Saleem's plot.

'You've got some wonderful things growing,' I reply, also whispering. 'What about your secret weapons, those carrots and parsnips in the drainpipes?'

'Ssh.' He taps his nose again. 'Ask no questions and you'll be told no lies.'

Some of my onions are falling over. They shouldn't be, because they are not ready yet and the leaves are still green, and I ask him what he thinks the trouble is. He lifts a couple and they came straight out of the ground with no need to pull. He turns them over and runs a thumb over the dry stubble which is all

135

that is left of their roots. There are small patches of white and green mould on the underside and one of the bulbs is going soft.

'Oh, no,' I say. 'Is that white rot?' This dreaded disease wiped out one of my first onion crops, and as it can stay dormant in the ground for twenty years, I have had to avoid that particular patch ever since.

'No,' he says. 'That's the bloody weather, too.'

A few minutes after he has gone I notice Five Pints hovering shyly on the path at the end of the trellis. I don't see him much because his plot is at the other end of the site and he comes and goes through a different gate, so I know this is not a chance encounter. 'How are you doing?' he asks.

'Fine,' I say and invite him on to the plot. He looks around making polite noises before getting to the purpose of his visit.

'I saw the Birdman here just now. Was he talking about the show?'

'Well . . .' This could be awkward. I don't want to be cast in the role of a go-between spy.

'Did he say anything about onions or dahlias?' I can happily answer this without feeling I am betraying any confidence.

'No. He was saying what a bad year it's been.' Five Pints nods solemnly at this. I ask: 'Are you putting much into the show?' The nod turns into a shake. 'No onions or dahlias?' He looks at me sharply, then remembers that he mentioned them first.

'Doubt it, the weather's not been right. I see you've got some good onions. Are you going to enter them?'

That is certainly why I grew the large varieties, and some of the bulbs are good, big and nicely shaped with glossy skins, but the caginess is catching. 'Well, I don't know. This weather . . .'. He nods again, understanding perfectly.

The onions whose leaves have collapsed have stopped growing and will not pick up again. The ripening process can be helped by pushing a fork under them and lifting so the roots are broken and they can lie on the surface, where the sun will dry them.

Thursday

Wait till the evening when it's cooler and pick two carrier bags of beans. I weigh them at home – 7 pounds – then set about preparing them for the freezer. The Viola Cornettis are simply topped and tailed and put whole into boiling water for two minutes to blanch. I know they are ready when they change colour from purple to dark green. It's a pity they lose their dramatic appearance and turn into ordinary-looking beans before they reach the table. The runners need more work before blanching, stripping the 'strings' from each side and slicing diagonally so that the immature beans inside the pods don't fall out. After cooling in cold water and drying they fill three large freezer bags.

Friday

The Ace Cultivator has put up a sign on his fence by the peaches which reads: 'DON'T EVEN THINK ABOUT IT.'

'Has it worked?' I ask.

'I think it has. Every time I counted them last week there were one or two missing, but since I put it up on Monday, none has gone. I think it makes people feel they are being watched. You must try one.' He goes along the branches testing the peaches to see if they are ripe by lifting them up a fraction in his palm and squeezing very gently. He finds one and twists it off and gives it to me. 'It's a Rochester.' I bite into the dark-red skin and it seems to explode with juice in my mouth. 'Good?' he asks. I can't speak with my mouth full so I roll my eyes with delight.

This has answered the question I was going to put to him about how I could tell when my Peregrines were ripe, but I still ask him to come and help me. There are just six peaches on my heavily pruned tree and Ace indicates two that he thinks are ready. I pick one and hold it in the palm of my hand. It is heavy and warm from the sun, and a pale-pink and yellow colour where his are a deep red. I rub the velvety skin against my lips to release the wonderful scent before biting into it slowly. Sweet juice spurts out and runs down my chin. It is unbelievably delicious and I close my eyes to savour every bit of the taste. When I open them Ace is laughing at me. I offer him the other peach but he shakes his head. He tests the greengages for me, Coe's Golden Drop and Cambridge Gage, and says they need another week or two.

We wander back to his plot and he shows me his Victoria plums which are ripe and a lovely mauve-blue, like the summer sky goes sometimes when a thunderstorm is about to break at dusk. The tree began as one of Saleem's suckers four years ago and it has prospered, unlike the one I planted. We try a few of them and agree that eating fruit perfectly ripe straight off the tree has to be one of life's great taste experiences. No chef could possibly improve on it.

I notice something odd about the Ace Cultivator's runner beans which I have seen somewhere else but can't remember where. Instead of the conventional support structure of poles in an inward-leaning A formation, either in rows or wigwams, his are leaning out at the top in a V shape. From a distance it reminds me of a pagoda.

'Do you know why?' he asks, reading my mind. 'The beans all hang freely, clear of the plants. This way they grow longer and straighter.' Some of them must be nearly a foot long. I ask if they are for the show and he shakes his head. 'I don't go in for competition.' Secretly pleased. He would win everything he entered.

I take the second peach home for my wife, wondering if this was the fruit which Eve tempted Adam with.

Saturday
Top up the frog pond with the hose, directing the water on to the overhanging rhubarb leaves so it comes down in a series of cascades. Three frogs rise to the surface, perhaps thinking it is raining. When I move the hose away on to the rhubarb crowns one of the frogs climbs out and hops after it as if wanting a shower.

Alan is sitting in the shade of his tree, which still hasn't produced apples despite his ultimatum to it, and I offer to fetch water for any plants that need it. His plot is too far from any of the taps for a hose to reach and he is too old to be carrying heavy cans of water any distance in this heat.

'Thanks, but no,' he says with a gentle smile. 'I think if you don't start to water them, they learn to cope without it. In fact, I think tomatoes have a much better flavour if they're kept on the dry side. I'd rather have small tasty ones than big bland watery ones.'

My runners seem to have stopped setting beans. Chicken Tom suggests spraying the flowers with sugar dissolved in water. 'The sugar will attract bees and they'll go into the flowers and pollinate them.' Like all his quirky ideas, it has a certain bizarre logic, but when I look more closely there don't seem to be that many flowers for the bees to pollinate. Saleem has spotted that as well.

'Pollination is not the problem,' he says. 'It's blackfly. Just look at it.' When I do, I see that the top sections of all the stems are black with flies and many leaves are beginning to shrivel. Why hadn't I noticed it before? Because my runner beans have never been attacked by blackfly before, so I wasn't looking for it.

'Where have they come from?' I ask in horror, and then I know. 'It was the broad beans, I bet. They were badly attacked earlier in the season and the flies must have migrated when the broad beans died down.' Even though I planted marigolds between the rows to deter aphids.

'So what are you going to do about it?' Saleem wants to know. He must be worried that the flies might migrate again, across the fence and on to his beans. Right now I haven't got an answer for him.

Sunday
Bring down half a bottle of liquid detergent and make up a strong solution in the sprayer. Spray up and down and side to side. The blackfly seem to be glued to the beans and the soapy water is running straight off them. Just like the broad beans, where soapy water had no effect whatsoever.

Saleem leans over the fence and sneers politely. 'It's no good washing them, you've got to kill them. If you don't get rid of them, you'll have no more beans.'

Max, sitting behind him in the doorway of the greenhouse, repeats soulfully: 'No more beans, mm-hm.'

'Those flies are sucking so much sap, the flower buds will never develop.'

'Sucking the sap, mm-hm.' Max sounds like the chorus in a Greek tragedy.

I allow myself to be led to the Trading Hut, where Saleem picks out a treatment. I begin: 'I'm organic . . .'

'I know, I know. This is all right.'

I try to read the label but I haven't brought my glasses, so I pass it back to him and ask: 'What does it say?'

He hasn't got his glasses, either, and holds it at arm's length. 'I don't know, but it's all right. Trust me.'

What choice do I have? I wait until the sun dries the beans, then spray them a second time with whatever is in the packet.

Monday

Ali is sitting at a table underneath a plum tree eating a lunch of bread, cheese, onion, apples, and other assorted fruit when I come through the gate by the Trading Hut and he waves me over with the knife he is holding. This is long and sharp with a slightly curved blade and, together with the scarf wrapped around his bald head to keep the sun off and the embroidered waistcoat worn without a shirt, makes him look like an ancient pirate or a mountain bandit, though not a dangerous one because he is laughing as always.

'My friend,' he chortles, 'look there.' He points briefly with the knife and then uses it to cut off a chunk of dark bread, a piece of cheese and a slice each of onion and apple, skewers them all together and proceeds to eat them off the blade. My tongue curls itself protectively against the roof of my mouth. When I look, I see a woman at the far end of the plot bent over a hoe. I immediately think it's the woman on the bus whom he persuaded to eat a raw onion and that he has charmed her with his garlic and other good things into coming to do some work for him.

'What's her name?' I ask with a smile.

'Not her,' he says dismissively. 'Is wife. Look there.' The knife points to a nearby framework of old iron gas pipes and wooden poles over which climbing plants are scrambling. 'I was tying blackberries on to pole when I find, guess what?' I'm not good at guessing, as I've just demonstrated, so I shake my head. 'Grape!' He utters the word triumphantly. I walk over to look and sure enough there is a vine growing up through the blackberries.

'And guess what? Is not there last year and I never plant, so mystery, eh? Like Agatha Christie.' He gestures for me to sit down on an upturned bucket and pushes a paper bag containing a bunch of grapes across the table towards me. 'Try. Very sweet. Very delicious.' He picks a handful himself. 'Is California Wonder from Mr Sainsbury. My favourite. Is so good I try to buy vine but no one sells it. I ask cousin in California and he sends cuttings last year but all die. Every day I sit here and eat my lunch and spit out pips on ground.' He spits pips into his hand and throws them towards the frame. 'And wish I grow grape.' He puts on a sad, clown's face and then a beaming happy one. 'And then up comes vine from pip. Mystery solved. Good, eh? And now.' He picks up a jar of olives and puts some in his mouth. 'I try for olive tree.' I'd better duck before he spits the stones out.

Wednesday
Inspect the sprayed beans. Many of the plants are clear of black-fly and the infestation on others is much reduced. Forgotten my glasses again and ask Alan, who has his on, to read the label on the packet Saleem gave me and tell me what he thinks. He has trouble with the long technical words, so he jumps to the end. 'It says it's safe to pick food crops after twenty-four hours, so it's probably organic, or close enough.' It's clearly potent stuff, so I give the beans another spray.

Harvest French beans, potatoes, courgettes, peas, lettuce and the first of the tomatoes, eating some of the small, cherry ones there and then with leaves stripped from the basil plant. The summer-fruiting raspberries are beginning to finish, though the new Autumn Bliss are covered in unripe berries. Still only a trickle of water from the tap, so no point in trying to use the hose. Leaves on the French beans and many other plants, including the rhubarb, are shrivelling for lack of water.

Thursday

Discover where it was I saw the pagoda-style bean frame before: on Five Pints plot. I'm coming in today from the church gates, having detoured to the off licence to buy a four-pack of ice-cold beer, and hear a saxophone playing mournfully. Go down a side path to follow it and it leads me to Five Pints. His plot is in amazingly good order – perhaps he comes down to water it at six in the morning – and I immediately notice the runner beans. They are immense. The saxophone stops, starts up on a long blaring note, then stops again. I'm about to walk away when the shed door opens and a large cider bottle is thrown clinking on to the rubbish heap I am standing beside. Five Pints blinks at me from the doorway, saxophone in hand. 'Whoops, sorry,' he says. 'I hope I didn't hit you.'

'No, it's all right. I was just admiring your beans, how long and straight they are.' They are even longer than the Ace Cultivator's. He puts the saxophone down inside the shed carefully and comes out.

'This variety is Enorma. Do you know why they are so straight?' I shake my head, and he carefully lifts one of the beans. A length of green twine is tied around the bottom of it and weighted at the other end by a small brass nut.

'Are they all like that?'

'I'd never have time to do all of them. Just the outstanding ones. You have to be careful not to mark the bean. I wrap a leaf around it before tying the twine on.'

'The show?' He nods. 'Where do you learn these tricks?' I ask in admiration.

'Looking and listening. Do you remember the talk by the show judge? He gave a lot away.'

I'd forgotten about that. 'Did he say anything about garlic and potatoes?'

'Yes.'

I rummage in the plastic bag and bring out the beer. 'Would you like a drink?' His face lights up. 'Now, about the garlic . . .'

Friday

Chicken Tom stops by and asks after my runner beans. Today he is wearing a hat with a fine net hanging from the brim, rather like a bee-keeper's but clearly home-made, probably from a curtain. 'To keep off flies,' he says. 'They're full of diseases. Did you know they vomit over their food?'

Grimace sympathetically and tell him the problem wasn't lack of pollination but damage by blackfly, preventing flower buds from developing, and now the blackfly is going I hope they will start to flower again. I thank him again for his suggestion about the sugar, and mention bird damage to the developing cobs of sweetcorn.

'Ah,' he cries, sufficiently interested to lift the net over the crown of the hat and clear of his face and kneel down to examine the cobs. He gets up. 'I had this problem last year but much worse. Come over and see what I've done.' Follow him to his plot. Behind the hen house there is a large plantation of corn of a different sort to mine – each plant is taller and carrying two or three cobs to my one. My Inner Saxon Peasant suffers a pang of corn envy.

'Last year was really bad,' he says. 'The cobs were growing lower down than these, nearly at ground level. Rooks were standing around as if they were at a royal garden party and doing their best to strip the lot. Not this year. Oh, no.' He takes a 2-litre plastic bottle from a bin liner full of them and unscrews the cap. Then he splits it lengthways with a folding pocket saw, leaving the base intact. He opens the bottle like crocodile jaws hinged at the bottom and slips it over a cob. It snaps shut with the narrow top fitting snugly over the stalk, enclosing the cob, yet providing room for it to grow as big as it wants.

'A beak-proof jacket,' I exclaim. 'Tom, that's brilliant.' He smiles modestly. 'Have you got any more ideas like that?'

'Oh, yes. I'm always inventing things in my shed. Have you seen my wind generator?' He points to the roof of his shed where a horizontal fan made from lengths of plastic guttering is spinning like a turbine on top of a pole. 'It drives an old car dynamo, which charges a couple of batteries in the shed. I can run lights and a television off them, and the parts cost me nothing. All scrap. Someone has asked me to make one powerful enough to run a computer.'

'What about a small fridge? Keep beer cold.'

He laughs. 'Maybe.'

All the plastic bottles I collected have been sunk into the ground beside plants to channel water to their roots, so I resort to a more traditional bird deterrent: a scarecrow. I have the plaster head of a shop-window mannequin which I found in a skip some time ago. Nail together two lengths of wood to make a cross, cover it with an old jacket and stuff with straw. Put the head on top with a Panama hat tied on to it, add one of my wife's scarfs around the neck, suspend a pair of shoes on wire below the jacket, then fix it into the ground on the edge of the corn. Stand back and admire. Hm. Good, but it needs something else.

Add an empty champagne bottle, and a red handkerchief in the top pocket. The face has a Mona Lisa-ish smile and as I am trying to think of a female name along the lines of Scarecrow Flo, or Baby Jo Scarecrow, Poppy comes along and says: 'I love your George Melly.'

'George Melly?' I step back to view it from her vantage point on the Ridgeway.

'Oh, yes,' she says. 'What about giving him a microphone to sing into?'

'Would it scare the rooks?'

'It might entice them.'

'No microphone, then.' Now she has put the idea into my head I can see the similarity. It's the smile. Or is it the hat? Anyway, George it is.

Saturday
The blackfly has gone from the runner beans and new flowers are opening. The French beans have stopped setting and the

leaves are turning yellow. I'm sure they have finished prematurely because of lack of water.

Pick the remaining four peaches and lightly prune the tree to shape it for next year. Cut out branches going in the wrong direction and tie the ones I want to keep on to bamboo canes angled across the trellis. Keep consulting the Ken Muir booklet, and at last I can see a resemblance between his illustrations and my tree.

Eat a couple of greengages as I work – a more delicate flavour than Victoria plums, and a finer, smoother texture. The tayberry which I planted against the trellis between the fruit trees has grown enormously since the spring, hidden behind the sweet peas, which are dying down. It has put out lateral branches 7 or 8 feet long to either side, about ten altogether. No fruit on them, as this is the first year, though the vigour promises basketloads of berries next year.

The only thing which hasn't done well against the trellis is the climbing rose I put in against a post at the shed end. It is barely hip high, with underdeveloped wood and few blooms. If it doesn't perk up by next spring, I will dig it out. There is no room here for sulky plants.

I've noticed Saleem eyeing my onions from his side of the fence, and he comes over and says: 'Some of those are nice. Are you going to put them into the show?'

'I don't know,' I say. It is two weeks yet, which seems too far away to start making a selection.

'Can I give you a tip? Put them somewhere warm and dark, like an airing cupboard or a garage. It will make the skins go brown and shiny. The judges like that.' Everyone seems to know what the judges like except me. What did I do with the notes I took at the lecture on showing?

Sunday
Encounter Carlo at the water tap. When fully turned on it just drips, and we fuel each other's anger at the unfair distribution of water and other people's selfishness.

He says, 'I was here the other day and that guy over there had his hose on this tap for seven hours. In the end I went over and said, "Don't you think it's somebody else's turn?" He wasn't in the least apologetic. Poppy and I have been forced to come down here at six in the morning to get enough water. If we didn't, half our plants would be dead by now.'

The demand for water is so great in a prolonged dry spell that the allotment pipes cannot cope. They have a small bore and have been tacked on to the end of the supply for a neighbouring street. Our tap is one of the last in the allotment network, literally right at the end of the line. We cast envious glances at better-placed plot holders holding hoses that gush like fountains. Carlo says some people have been threatening to sabotage the lucky ones.

Will history record that the global conflict over diminishing water resources which is expected to blight the twenty-first century began with a punch-up over whose turn it was with a tap on a certain allotment site in England? Probably not, but it may be true all the same.

Monday
The swifts and swallows which have been gathering on telephone lines in increasing numbers for the past few weeks have suddenly gone, back to Africa. My heart sinks, because their departure marks the beginning of the end of summer, even though the days are still long and hot. In the evening the peals of bell practice from St Jude's Church make me stop in the middle of bagging up the onions to take home. I always think of that as a winter sound, and a comforting one on a cold, dark night, but now it is another sign that the year is turning.

For a moment I feel sad, then give myself a shake. I won't let summer go yet. There could be weeks and weeks of it to come, and I will enjoy every moment of it while I can.

September

It rains. At last. I feel a great sense of relief, as if my own roots have been parched for weeks past. It is a slow, steady, drenching rain which falls from a sky as flat and featureless as a grey blanket. It is raining when I get up in the morning and has been for hours, judging by the puddles in the street and the dark stains on the trunks of trees. I imagine the thirsty earth gulping it down. Give the allotment a miss and stay indoors plaiting onions into strings around a central core of binder twine. It is a fiddly job which takes hours. Try the same with garlic, but the leaves are more brittle and break easily. It is better to put them in the small

147

red net bags some supermarkets use to package vegetables which I keep for this purpose.

Hang a dozen long onion strings and three bags of garlic from roof struts in the garage, where good ventilation should prevent them rotting. It's a fine sight which hugely pleases my Inner Saxon Peasant and his need to store up the summer's feast against winter's famine. I hold back ten of the best onions as possible show entries, the ones that weigh about 2 pounds each, and also a dozen or so others that won't keep, either because their skin is damaged or their necks are thick, which means they will go soft soon.

It is still raining when I go to bed, and the warm air is soggy with humidity.

Wednesday
Still raining. The puddles in the street are joining up where the drains are blocked and the day is dim and depressing. Peel and pickle shallots, adding my own hot peppers to the vinegar to give it spiciness, and make onion relish from some of the damaged bulbs. This is a lovely relish which can be served hot or cold with almost anything, and will keep in a jar in the fridge for weeks, if it gets the chance. I have some of it as a topping on a cheese and ham sandwich for lunch.

Onion Relish
Cut two or three large onions into medium thick rings, cook in olive oil with a generous amount of rosemary for ten minutes until they darken, add two glasses of white wine and half a glass of wine vinegar, two tablespoons of brown sugar, a little salt and pepper, and simmer until the liquid is absorbed – about an hour. Store in screw-top jars. For a variation in taste, a dessert-spoon of ginger can be added with the sugar.

The rain has lessened to a fine drizzle. The whole world looks soaked and bedraggled and the allotment will be a quagmire, so I retrieve the demijohns of wine from the dining-room cupboard and set them out on the kitchen table, taking the precaution of laying down plenty of newspaper. Both the apple and the elderflower are clear and sharp to look at, though there is a thin layer of fine sediment in the bottom of all the jars which rises slightly as I put them down. The light passing through the apple has a warm, sunset-like tint and the elderflower is a lighter straw colour.

While the sediment settles I wash and dry thirty bottles which have been stored in the garage. I will rack the wine off into them through a plastic tube, leaving the sediment behind, but first I must find out what the wine is like by tasting a quarter of a glassful from each jar. This is a tense moment, the stage at which my father used to fulminate against the dreaded vinegar fly which would dive into his wine if he left a cork off for half a minute and ruin it. I was never sure whether it existed or if it was a mythical insect which could be conveniently blamed if anything went wrong, as wine is a contrary thing which spoils very easily. He began to dose his wine with more and more sulphurous chemicals to ward the fly off, making some of it undrinkable, but his elderflower was legendary in the family for its delicious flavour. This wine is just flowers or fruit, water, sugar and yeast; nothing else.

The first elderflower is dry and sharp, with an overly strong flavour. The second and third are equally dry, though milder, so they should be blended with the first. All are rather light in body because they are made from flowers, and would probably be best as an aperitif, before moving on to something more assertive with food.

I know the apple is going to be completely different as soon as I decant some. The bouquet bursts out of the glass and fills the kitchen. It tastes like apples which have been soaked in honey then cooked slowly with nuts and orange peel. It is wonderful, even though it is much sweeter than I normally like. The other jars are equally good, varying only in the amount and degree of sweetness. The wine is mouth-filling and heart-warming. It transforms the day, dispelling the gloom and bringing the sun into the kitchen and a smile to my lips.

By the time I have blended the elderflower for dryness and the apple for sweetness and tasted it again, I am quite befuddled. When the rest of the family come home, the table is covered in bottles, the floor is awash with spilled wine, and I am happily humming to myself while trying to write labels but finding it impossible to get the words to fit on the small squares of paper.

Thursday
The wine was pure and I have no hangover this morning, which is just as well because the rain has stopped, the sun is shining and there is work to catch up with.

When I open the allotment gates, I can see the rain has had an immediate tonic effect. The plants have lost their dusty, slightly bleached and droopy appearance. Everything is greener, more upstanding. Even the grass.

The Birdman is up to something in his greenhouse as I pass and shout a greeting. He waves to me to come in. He is sorting through a pile of onions, rubbing off the outer skins and grading them with the help of an ancient set of grocer's scales with brass weights which look like large chess pieces.

'What do you think of those?' he asks, holding out two whoppers, one in each hand.

'Wow,' I say faintly, feeling a surge of onion envy from my Inner Saxon Peasant.

'How heavy would you say they were?'

'Um, er.' They are so much bigger than mine, the ones I thought would be contenders for a prize, that I am lost for words.

'Six pounds. Each. Not bad, eh?' He laughs in delight.

'Not bad,' I repeat, trying to hide my disappointment. 'Are these the ones I gave you as seedlings after your greenhouse was burned down?'

'No, they didn't amount to anything. I think you started them off too late.' His face clouds for a moment. 'I've heard that Five Pints has some which are even bigger.'

'Even bigger?' Could that be possible? 'What variety are they?'

'Stuttgart Giant.'

'I grew those and they're not a patch on yours.'

'Ah, but did you buy the special mammoth seed?' he asks with his crafty smile.

'No. What about your carrots and parsnips?'

'Ah.' The smile widens. 'I'm not going to lift those until the day of the show. Spring a surprise on everyone. I'll need it. The dahlias and chrysanthemums are a disaster.' They are not the only ones. I sense something wrong as soon as I stop on the Ridgeway to give my plot a quick overview. The pumpkin I was growing for the children for Hallowe'en has split down the side and all the ripening tomatoes have burst. It's the rain. After weeks of drought they have gorged themselves on water, swelled up and 'Splat!'.

Oddly, the unripe tomatoes are all right. Perhaps green skins can stretch more easily than red ones. Some of the burst tomatoes are already infected with rot and have to be thrown on to the compost. The rest can be salvaged if I gather them immediately and either turn into soup or pulp and freeze.

Leave the pumpkin. May be able to incorporate the split into a face later on. A lot of the berry fruit has been knocked to the ground and spoiled and the lettuces have bolted, suddenly growing up in columns to flower and set seed. When this happens they become too bitter to eat. Worried about the sweetcorn in case the kernels have burst, too. Don't look, as this means peeling back the skins which will spoil them.

There is one consolation. The beans loved the rain. The climbing French have been revitalised, and there are scarlet flowers all over the runners and a mass of tiny new pods.

Friday

The surface of the soil has dried out already, though it is damp just underneath. There is a tight little knot of people a couple of plots away towards the railway line studying something, and I drift over to be nosy. When I join them I see they are staring at a hole in the ground and that wasps are coming and going from it in a constant stream.

The Ace Cultivator tells me that the tenant, Maisie, has been stung twice and is terrified of being stung again. She has appealed for someone to get rid of the nest and is staying at home until it is made safe.

Saleem has a puffer of poisonous powder and the Birdman has a can of petrol. Confucius says, 'Why not just ask the wasps to go away? They do that, you know. I tried it with caterpillars and it worked.' No one takes any notice of this, but nor do they inquire if he has had a sudden increase in butterflies and moths. I ask if he ever managed to get a bee hive going. 'Yes, a small one. It's behind my shed, hidden in an old water tank. No one knows it's there. I think.'

Five Pints arrives with a can of paraffin, and a debate starts over the best treatment. The powder is dismissed as too slow-acting.

'This will dissolve their wings,' says Five Pints, lifting the paraffin can.

'Ah, but this will incinerate the buggers,' counters the Birdman.

'But isn't it dangerous?' I ask. 'And won't you get stung as you stand there pouring it in?'

'Not if someone is ready with a burning rag on the end of a stick and jams it in the hole quickly.'

'What if it goes off with a bang and blows the nest into the air? There could be a lot of very angry wasps around here.'

'You worry too much,' says the Birdman, but I notice that the others have moved away a bit and I follow them. Five Pints wraps newspaper around the end of a bamboo cane, splashes paraffin on it and lights it. The Birdman takes the top off his can, drops it on to the ground at the edge of the hole and steps back while it empties itself into the nest. Wasp activity round the hole is increasing by the second. 'Are you ready?' he shouts as he goes forward to kick the empty can out of the way.

'Damn! Hang on a second,' cries Five Pints. The paper has gone out. It was still damp from the rain. He pours more paraffin on to it and it lights by itself from a red ember with a whoosh which singes his eyebrows. 'Bloody hell!' he yells.

'Come on, come on!' shouts the Birdman, dancing around to dodge wasps and slapping the air. Five Pints shoves the burning paper into the hole. There is an explosive whump as the petrol vapour ignites and the shock wave from the blast smacks me in the face. Flames shoot high into the air. The blast hasn't ejected any wasps, though ones which are returning from foraging try to fly into the nest despite the fire and are burned up in the flames. When the fire dies down we go up to inspect the damage. The hole has been enlarged and the earth around it is scorched. It is like a miniature bomb crater, dotted with dead wasps.

'That's sorted them out,' says the Birdman, rubbing the back of his left hand. 'I'll give Maisie the all clear.' He turns to Five Pints. 'Next time keep the blooming paper burning and I might not get stung.'

'Sorry,' mutters Five Pints. He is running his fingertips over his eyebrows to see how much of them are left. Well, I was right about one thing. It was dangerous. And the competition between these two has already started.

Saturday
The show is a week away and people have started behaving strangely. Some saunter about the place trying too hard to be casual, or loiter on paths pretending to have lost their way. Others who are normally open and friendly are now evasive and secretive or hiding away in their sheds.

The first lot aren't vegetable rustlers casing the joint, they are contestants sizing up the competition, and the second lot are one step further on and getting their entries ready. I will wait till the last minute before deciding what to enter to let the full effects of the recent downpour work through everything.

In the Trading Hut Queeny has marshalled the Hut Ladies to help her label jars of jam. She is putting a hundred up for sale on a stall at the show to raise funds for the Allotment Association. They are all made from allotment fruit donated by friends. We reminisce about the last show and I complain about my sloe gin being disqualified. She comes up with a brilliant idea, revealing a talent for low cunning I had never suspected before.

'Why not enter it under preserved fruit, or pickles?' She leafs through the rule book. 'There is nothing here which says pickles have to be in vinegar or restricted to onions and other vegetables.'

The ladies giggle. 'It would be a bit of a laugh,' says one.

'Give those stuffy old men something to think about,' says another. I think she means the judges, or is it the competitors? It would, anyway. It certainly would.

When I return to my plot, Stu is standing on the Ridgeway photographing it, or rather George.

'We've decided to run a scarecrow competition,' he says. 'They've been springing up all over the place. Have you noticed?' I hadn't. 'Yes. This is the fifth one I've photographed today. I'll put the pictures on the web page and in the next newsletter and invite people to vote for the one they like the most.'

'What's first prize?' I ask.

'We haven't got that far.' He packs his camera away. 'They're all very different, you know. Some are quite bizarre and weird. I have a theory that they all resemble the people who made them.' I look critically at George, who has developed a tilt to one side, making the Mona Lisa-ish smile look more like a drunken leer. Stu adds as he leaves: 'Perhaps I shouldn't pursue that theory.' Perhaps not.

George seems to be losing his stuffing. Bits of straw are on the ground around him. Have a nasty suspicion that Chicken Tom's canny rooks or Magic's starlings have worked him out for the dummy he is and are pulling him to bits. But why? They are not building nests at this time of year.

Middy hurries by to the tank with her watering can. 'Surely nothing needs watering after all that rain?' I say.

She shakes the can. 'Pee. Lots of lovely nitrogen for the tomatoes.'

'Oh, right. What are you putting into the show?'

'Nothing. I seem to be in a between stage. I've harvested half my stuff and the other half won't be ready until afterwards.'

The Artist stops and says: 'I know. It's the same with me.' She rolls her eyes in exasperation. 'Do you think if I did paintings of tomatoes and cabbages and things I could put them in as exhibits?'

Magic is lifting all his tomatoes, including the green ones, because he has heard that tomato blight is spreading across the site from plots by the church. He has at least a hundred plants, which must mean three or four hundred pounds of tomatoes and he doesn't want to risk losing them. He says he will ripen them at home on windowsills.

As the afternoon slips into evening, Sailor and the Ace Cultivator come by and invite me to join them for a drink at the Fox and Ferret. We meander across the site to the church gates, stopping frequently to comment on the state of other people's plots. We get our pints and take them through into the beer garden to enjoy the warm dusk and are no sooner settled than the Hon. Sec. bustles into the garden, looking businesslike with a clipboard in one hand and a tankard in the other.

'Now then,' he says. 'There's a bit of a crisis on the stewarding front for next week. Half the people who did it last year have dropped out for one reason or another.' What I've actually heard in the Hut is that he retired the oldest and most doddery, who were so slow last year that the end of the judging was delayed by nearly an hour, and some of the others, who have been doing it for fifty years, got huffy and resigned in solidarity.

'I've put you three down for . . .'. He looks at the clipboard.

'Not me,' says Ace quickly. 'I'm away for the day, taking my wife shopping.'

The Hon. Sec. gives him a withering look. 'Taking your wife shopping?' He makes it sound like a form of social deviance.

'It's her birthday.'

'Her birthday?' I almost expect him to add: 'That's no excuse.' 'You mean you're not entering the show?'

Ace hangs his head and mutters unhappily, 'No.'

'Well. I thought you would be one of our best competitors. I do think that the really good gardeners have a duty to enter to raise the standard and encourage others by showing what good crops can be grown. I really do.'

'Sorry.' The word is almost inaudible.

The Hon. Sec. glares at him, then turns briskly to Sailor. 'Setting up exhibits or cataloguing the results?'

'Anything, I don't mind,' says Sailor from behind a cloud of Navy Cut tobacco smoke.

The Hon. Sec. turns to me, waving the smoke away and I cough ingratiatingly as it engulfs me. 'You've not done it before, so I've given you something easy. Escorting a judge. Any preference? Vegetables, domestics, flowers?' I shake my head as I don't know what the job involves anyway. 'Good.' He empties the tankard at a gulp and gets up. A thought occurs to me.

'I can still compete, can I?'

'Good heavens, yes. Same again, everyone?' He points to our glasses.

'I mean, no one's worried that I could influence the judge towards my exhibits, are they?' I'm speaking to his retreating back as he heads for the bar, and Sailor answers with a laugh.

'No. But you could try it, anyway.'

Ace says, 'I've never gone in for the show, he knows that. I'm just not the competitive type. I can't help it.'

'I'm sure no one minds,' I say. 'He was just trying to fill the jobs and using press-gang tactics to do it.'

'The show's only a bit of fun,' adds Sailor. I am beginning to have doubts about that. It is all getting rather serious.

Sunday
Search high and low for the notes I took at the talk given by the show judge ages ago. I remember he had lots of brilliant tips, but not what they were. Go through the pockets of all my allotment clothes and ransack the cupboard drawers where all the odds and ends finish up. It puts me in a bad temper when I can't find them, and I stomp off to the allotment late in the afternoon to work it off with some aggressive hoeing.

Then I prepare a new bed for garlic, forking over the soil and removing weeds. Dress with well-rotted compost and rake under the surface and firm the soil by treading it down. Break up three garlic bulbs into individual cloves and plant. Will do more next month.

When I put the tools away, I discover the notes, rolled up and

pushed into a clean jam jar on a shelf inside the shed where I must have put them so they wouldn't get damp or be chewed up for bedding by mice. Mood lifts instantly. Settle down on the sun lounger under the vine to read them. Remember now the tip on picking individual beans when they are just right and keeping them fresh in the fridge wrapped in cling film until the day. Ah, here's one on plumping up marrows and pumpkins by threading a wick into their stalks from a jar of sugar water. It's probably too late to try that. I wish I'd remembered it earlier.

I look up from the notes when I can no longer read them in the twilight and see two foxes dancing around each other on Saleem's plot like a couple of boisterous puppies. They know I am here but are quite unconcerned and ignore me. I feel I am the intruder, that with the approach of night the allotments are moving out of the human domain and into an animal one. Gather my things together and creep away so as not to disturb them.

Tuesday
Lift some carrots to see what they are like. The leafy tops are not big so I have left them alone, thinking the roots were still growing, but they have been in the ground a long time and should be ready.

157

The fork comes up with a collection of monsters. Not 'monsters' as in big, but carrots which have been twisted and knotted into monstrous shapes. Some are tightly corkscrewed, some forked into three, four or five fingers, and others distorted into vaguely human or animal forms. Many of them are split and have opened out like thick books. Nearly all of them have ragged holes near the top where the carrot fly has eaten into them.

They look so awful I can't consider eating them, let alone exhibiting them. But that is totally out of the question in any case. I fork up the lot and throw them into a heap to take to the compost bin, reluctant even to touch any of them as if they might come alive in my hand. Saleem peers over the fence and says, 'Yuck.'

'Yeah, right. I don't know what happened.'

He comes round and pokes through the heap. 'You know what caused that? Your soil is too rich. You've been dressing it with manure and feeding it with fertiliser and it just makes carrots go crazy. They need thin, sandy soil. Hungry soil.'

'That's a relief,' I say. 'I was beginning to think they were alien spawn or something.'

He goes back to his plot and returns with a handful of carrots each about 10 inches long, as straight as a ruler and unblemished. 'Here. I grew these under the apple trees where the soil is poor.'

'Those are beauties. You're bound to win with those.'

'No, these are my rejects. The ones for the show are much better.'

I think I may give up growing carrots altogether. This is bad for my self-esteem. At least the tomatoes are now producing well.

Wednesday

There is a good flush of blackberries on the wild brambles growing along the railway cutting. Pick about 5 pounds and ignore all the scratches from the thorns. I remember brambling expeditions with my cousins when I was a child; we would collect baskets of fruit from country lanes and my mother would turn them into blackberry and apple pies with sugar-speckled pastry which melted in the mouth. I used to tell her that she was the best 'cooker' in the world. 'Gas or electric?' she'd say, and everyone would laugh.

The beans are cropping again with great vigour. They are growing so quickly that by the time I have worked to the end of a row and filled a plastic bag, I could almost go back to the beginning and start picking afresh. Weigh them at home. Fourteen pounds of runners and 6 pounds of French. Put some aside for mother- and sisters-in-law and slice, blanch and pack the rest into freezer bags. The freezer is rapidly filling up and I will have to give more away to neighbours. The Ace Cultivator once told me that he does not have a freezer and when I asked what he did with his surplus produce, he hummed and hawed a bit before admitting that he gave it away to needy people, mostly old age pensioners. I think quite a few others do, too, and say nothing about it.

Thursday

Thieves have stolen Saleem's potato crop. Most of it, anyway. He is sitting on the ground against his greenhouse looking stunned when I arrive after breakfast and I go straight over to ask what the matter is, thinking he may be ill. He points and makes a strangled sound. The potato bed looks as if someone has driven a plough through it. The ground is churned up and the tall haulms have been uprooted and thrown down on the ground any old how.

Rita comes trudging up the path. She has been on the phone to the Manager and the police from a neighbour's house. 'There's nothing they can do,' she says bitterly. We go over to the bed. Here and there is a large, dark potato which has been overlooked in the thieves' hurry. They are Desiree, a main crop with a reddish skin which are equally good boiled, baked, roasted or chipped.

'They must have been up here at 5.30,' says Saleem. 'Dug up as much as they could and got away before they were disturbed.'

Rita says: 'Someone bringing the milk in thought they saw them loading sacks into a van at the gates but didn't think twice

about it. People sometimes come to water very early before going on to work.'

'Bastards!' groans Saleem.

'I'm sorry,' I say, knowing it's no comfort.

'You know what the worst thing is?' says Saleem, almost in tears. 'It's that this was done by people from here, almost certainly people I know, because they must have had a key to the gates. You don't climb over a fence with a sack of potatoes on your back.'

'Why?' I ask helplessly, as I did when the Birdman's greenhouse was burned down by vandals. Potatoes are not exactly a luxury crop, nor are they scarce or expensive. You can buy a half-hundredweight sack from the local greengrocers for £5.

'Jealousy,' snaps Rita.

'Or,' says Saleem, 'they were stealing to order for a restaurant or a shop which can charge a high price for organic potatoes.'

I came down today to draw up my final list of entries for the show, but this has greatly depressed me. Being under attack by thieves and vandals from outside is one thing. Being robbed by fellow allotmenteers is the worst of treacheries.

Go into my shed and close the door and rummage through my little stock of books until I find *Allotments* by R.P. Lister, a book of poems and thoughts about allotments illustrated with wood engravings by Miriam Macgregor. The poems are rather unsophisticated, unlike the powerful 'John Maydew, or The Allotment' by Charles Tomlinson, but the pictures are brilliant. They are full of sly humour and sharp observation, and as I turn the pages my gloom lifts and I cheer up.

The entry form has to be given to the Hon. Sec. tomorrow, so I must get on with it. Put the book back and start a tour of inspection with form in hand. All the beans are looking good, so circle Classes 8 and 9, respectively nine pods of runner and French beans. The Pink Fir Apples have also done well after the rain, so circle Class 6, four potatoes, coloured and named, staged on a plate. On through the classes for capsicums, onions under 8 ounces, tomatoes, sweetcorn.

This is getting intoxicating. Biggest Marrow In Show? You bet. Selection Of Fruit? Why not? Chutney, pickles, jelly jam? Yes, yes, yes. Aubergines, beetroot, cucumber . . . wait a minute. Did I grow any?

Sit down and force myself to be sensible, which means going through the entry form again and changing a lot of things. Chew my pencil and agonise and change a few more. What have I got now? About ten entries, which is not many as the competition runs to 115 classes. I have cut back too much. Surely I can enter more than ten without getting carried away?

Study the form again, and wonder if this is where the racing expression comes from, 'studying form'. Only thirty of the classes are for vegetables and a mere five for fruit. There are twenty in the domestic section for cakes, jams and preserves, and seven for beer and wine. The rest are for flowers, mostly dahlias and chrysanthemums.

Now I discover something which has not registered with me in previous years because I don't grow competition flowers, only marigolds and nasturtiums to deter aphids, sweet peas to cut for the house, sunflowers for the birds and a rose scrambling over the trellis. Of the thirty silver cups and trophies, twenty-one are for flowers. There are six for vegetables and three for domestics.

Digger's Diary

This seems very strange. We are not a floral society, after all. The rules of many allotment associations actually forbid the cultivation of flowers in case they are grown commercially. Their middle-class Victorian patrons insisted that allotments were to provide food for working-class families only and not be a source of income which might give them too much independence.

It means that any serious trophy hunter at the show must go into flowers in a big way. Why dahlias and chrysanthemums? I don't like either. Dahlias are so often overblown and blowsy, a barmaidy sort of flower, and chrysanthemums always make me think of funerals. I must ask the Hon. Sec. if he can spread the trophies around a bit. There's not a single one for fruit. My peaches would have deserved a cup – if I hadn't eaten them all. But there is always next year.

Friday

Take the completed entry form round to the Hon. Sec.'s house and he invites me in for a cup of tea. He is in the middle of preparing his own exhibits and the large sitting room is crammed full of goodies, covering nearly all the floor space and most of the furniture. There are crates of bottled beers and wine and several full 5-gallon plastic fermenting vessels still to be racked off. There is a laundry basket of onions, a log basket of shallots, sacks of potatoes, a pyramid of large creamy cauliflowers, trusses of tomatoes cascading over a sofa, glass jars of all sizes holding preserves and chutneys, two low tables stacked with trays of cakes, tarts, flans and biscuits, and more cut flowers in vases than a wedding. Everywhere I look there is more. Cabbages, leeks, parsnips, chard. Apples, damsons, strawberries, pears.

'Have a seat,' he says, sitting himself down on a pouffe drawn up at a third table where he is wrapping red raffia round an inch of leaf stub on a matched set of onions. I look around but there aren't any which are unoccupied. He pushes tomatoes into a cardboard box so that I can sit on the edge of the sofa. His wife comes in looking hot but cheerful and bringing a waft of baking smells from the kitchen, including warm cinnamon and apple with cloves. She puts more trays of cakes on a table and hurries back to her oven.

'Is this all yours?' I ask. It's rather a stupid question, but there is so much of everything it is hard to believe that one allotment – actually, two in his case – could have produced it all.

'Sure is.' He positions the set of onions on a dish spread with white sand. The sand keeps them neatly in place; otherwise they would all sit differently and untidily on the dish. My exhibits currently occupy just half the kitchen table at home, though there are some I won't collect from the allotment until tomorrow morning so that they will be as fresh as possible.

'Blimey. How many exhibits have you got?'

'Oh, about eighty-five. I've been preparing them for a week.' He discards one of the onions and selects another from the laundry basket, clips its leaves and starts to tape the stub with raffia.

'Do you have to do all that?' I ask. I'm worried. I was just planning to cut the leaves short on mine and leave them like that.

There's a sharp intake of breath. 'Of course. Presentation is vital. It makes your exhibit stand out from the crowd and catches the judge's eye. If there is nothing to choose between two or more exhibits in quality, then this will make all the difference.' The Hon. Sec. arranges the onions to his satisfaction, puts them down and lifts two beer bottles out of a crate. 'Now, look at that. It's stout. I haven't made it before and I thought, I won't get any ordinary bottles, I'll use old-fashioned ones with thick brown glass and these wire-clip stoppers instead of metal caps.'

'Impressive.'

'It's presentation, you see. Of course, what really counts is the stout. Let's taste it.' He deftly opens a bottle by pressing the clip with his thumb. There's a hiss and white foam climbs out of the neck. He opens the other one and pours the stout into two glasses. We raise the glasses and rotate them to see how the light passes through.

'It's a good colour,' I say, 'with a lovely head.' It has the rich darkness of black coffee. The foam on top lies thick, like a layer of cream. Together we lift our glasses and drink and smack our lips. 'Excellent.'

'Mm,' he murmurs, 'not bad. Not bad at all, at all,' putting on an Irish accent. When we finish the stout, he says we should try the pale ale for the contrast.

'Should we be drinking the exhibits?' I ask. 'Don't you need them for the show?'

He waves a hand airily. 'Don't worry, I've got a cellar full downstairs.'

I forget to raise the matter of the flower trophies. When I set off home some time later, I decide to redo all my exhibits with a bit more showmanship. Stop on the way to get raffia and white sand from the D.I.Y. shop, then to the allotment to pick vine leaves to use as decorative plate coverings under the exhibits. Pick a handful of raspberry leaves as well, because the spear shape with serrated edges looks so interesting.

The Birdman is sitting on a chair beside the open door of his shed looking tired. 'Got everything ready for tomorrow?' I ask.

'Just about,' he says. I start to tell him about Saleem's potatoes, but he has already heard.

'It's a bad business, and it's nothing to do with selling to restaurants. He's been nobbled by the competition.'

'What?'

'Saleem's potatoes have won for the last four years. Someone has got fed up with losing to him, so they've made sure he won't win this year. I wouldn't be surprised if Saleem's potatoes turn up under somebody else's name.'

'How would anyone know?'

'Ah, that's the trouble. They wouldn't. Which is why I slept here last night and will again tonight to make sure no one steals my carrots and parsnips. And if they try . . .'. He leans into the doorway and brings out a long-barrelled pistol.

My eyes pop. 'Hey, you can't go shooting people over a carrot,' I squeak in genuine alarm.

'Don't worry. It's not a real gun. It's one of those paintball things they use for corporate-leadership games. I got it from my son. I've filled the balls with quick-drying red dye which will only come off with half a gallon of nail-polish remover. If I hit anyone with this, they'll be walking about like a flaming tomato for days.'

He has rigged up an alarm system of wires and bells around his carrots and parsnips, connected to a floodlight powered by a car battery. On the way to the gate I hear a saxophone swinging. I bet Five Pints is also staying the night to watch over his beans.

Redoing the exhibits fancily takes me half the night. The Hon. Sec. made it look easy to tie off an onion with raffia. I am all fingers and thumbs trying to do it with a dozen small shallots and five garlic bulbs. The raffia keeps unravelling and I simply cannot tie a knot in it. My wife suggests stitching it together with thread of the same colour, but that would be even more fiddly. Stick the ends down with glue instead. Stagger upstairs as the church clock strikes two and look out of the bedroom window towards the dark allotments and wonder what's going on down there now.

Saturday
Show Day. I should be leaping out of bed first thing, but have to be elbowed out by my wife because I am so tired. Open the curtains and it's raining. Oh, no. This never entered my calculations. It will ruin all the things I was going to pick last thing, like the beans. I can't compete with Five Pints on straightness as I didn't weight the pods, so I had hoped to make up for it with ultra-freshness.

Saturday morning is usually one of the busiest times, but there is no one around as I hurry through the gates and up the path. The Birdman has flown and his carrot and parsnip pipes are empty, but did he take them or did someone else? Within seconds of starting to pick runner beans I am soaked. Water has gathered in the cupped leaves and it pours off the dense foliage every time I grope for a bean. First I try to grade them for length and shape and pick only the ones which will match up, but this doesn't work, so I pick all the longest ones to sort through later.

165

The church clock strikes ten and I realise with a rush of panic that there is hardly any 'later' left. All the exhibits have to be delivered to the church hall and set up on the benches by noon. The doors close at 12.15 sharp and judging begins in private at 12.30.

Move on to the French beans and collect some nice specimens, but in my haste the pruning knife slips on a wet stalk and slices into the ball of my thumb. It is very sharp and blood pours down my hand. Get some clean kitchen towel from the shed to staunch the blood then put on a garden glove to keep it in place. No time to stop. On to the sweet peppers, which have done well in the shelter of the sweetcorn. I need three for an exhibit and when I checked them two days ago, there were four large ones ripening to a bright red. Disaster. There are slugs on all of them and when I shake them off, see that two of the peppers are badly holed, so I won't have enough to exhibit. There are long red Cayenne peppers growing alongside them which the slugs have ignored. I'll enter those instead and hope the judges don't notice, and if they do, say 'Well, they're all capsicums'.

Must hurry. Pick half an ice-cream carton of Autumn Bliss raspberries, dropping quite a few of them because of the glove. Only need fifteen, but I want plenty to choose from because there is quite a colour variation and many of them are so ripe the berries are falling off the stalks – any in that state will be disqualified. What else? Can hardly see because rain is running down the inside as well as the outside of my glasses. My trousers are sticking to my legs and rain has seeped inside the collar of my waxed jacket and made my shirt clammy against my back. Will have to get back in time to change, or I'll catch a chill if I have to stay in wet clothes all afternoon for the stewarding.

The first bong of 11 o'clock booms from the church tower. That's it. Must go. Wait a minute. The marrows. Quickly cut the two I earmarked for a pair days ago and in trying to shove them both into one plastic bag split it and they fall out. Are they damaged? Can't see. Stagger down the path and through the gates with five heavy bags banging against my knees and go home to change, bandage the cut and make a final selection of beans and berries.

The rain has stopped and the sun is out when I get to the church hall. It is like a railway station in the rush hour, with people milling about in all directions. Arrive late at ten past twelve, only five minutes before the doors are shut. If I wasn't a steward and able to stay on inside the locked hall, I would not have enough time to set everything up. Collect the numbered cards which go with every entry and pay the fee for each one: ten pence. Have managed to muster fifteen entries, though some are very iffy.

When I go into the main hall, I see the Birdman moving away from a bench with a dazed smile on his face. He has just laid out his sets of three carrots and three parsnips, which completely dwarf all the other entries in their classes. I have never seen anything like them. They are immensely long. 'How big are they?' I ask him. He looks dazed, I think, because the full realisation of his achievement has only just hit him after seeing his vegetables alongside the rest. There is no doubt, even before the judging starts, that those carrots and parsnips will sweep the board.

'My secret weapons?' he says. 'The parsnips are 28½ inches and the carrots are 25 inches.'

'Unbelievable.'

'What have you done to your hand?' Blood is soaking through the bandage; I should probably have gone to Casualty to have the cut stitched up. I explain, showing him the pruning knife with its wickedly curved blade. 'You should do what I do with a deep cut. Forget doctors. Get a tube of Superglue, run it along the cut and press the two sides together. Always works.' Feel queasy at the thought of it.

The Hon. Sec. and the other stewards are clearing the building and I quickly put out my entries. By the time I finish, the main hall is empty of people but full of produce, and I stand back to take it all in. It is a wonderful sight. At one end are banks of flowers in vases and pots, not just dahlias and chrysanthemums but sunflowers, roses, asters, fuchsias, gladioli, carnations and many more in clouds of colour and scent. Ranged around the room and across it are benches almost buckling beneath the weight of fruit and vegetables.

And what fruit and vegetables. Not simply big and clean and unblemished, but beautifully proportioned and matched. They radiate healthiness.

The domestic section is at the end opposite the flowers. Tables of mouth-watering cakes and pies, bread and scones, quiches and flans, not as much wine and beer as I expected but hundreds of jars and bottles of jam, jelly, chutney and pickles. My black-currant jam in Class 54 for soft fruit is up against twenty-seven others. The competition there is going to be very tough. To give it an edge, move my jar to the front and flounce up the 'bonnet' my wife made for it from an old Laura Ashley patterned skirt.

Among the beautifully clear exhibits in the honey class along-side is one jar which stands out. It is murky and full of bits, of comb I suppose, and also parts of dead bees. Turn the card over. Confucius. He probably thinks filtering honey is unnatural and spoils the flavour.

I am summoned by the Hon. Sec. and go through the double doors into the entrance hall to have my steward's badge pinned to my lapel. The hatches are being raised on the busy, steaming kitchen womanned by Queeny and the Hut Ladies, and sliding doors to two side rooms have been pushed back. The scrutineers are setting up in one to record the judgements and unpacking boxes of trophies, and a long table is being laid in the other where the committee and stewards will entertain the judges to lunch after their work is done.

I am struck by the air of professional competence. Everyone is taking this very seriously. The Hon. Sec. has even foregone his Bermuda shorts in favour of a suit. So much for Sailor and the Birdman calling it 'only a bit of fun'.

Almost expect a fanfare when the judges arrive at the grave-yard door and are ushered in. There are three of them, a man and two women from neighbouring allotment societies who have been approved as judges by the Royal Horticultural Society. They will each take one of the three sections.

'Which one do you want to work with?' the Hon. Sec. asks me.
'I don't know.'
'What have you mostly entered?' asks Sailor.
'Vegetables.'
'Join me and we'll escort Madam Judge there, doing vegetables and fruit.' She has already begun a preliminary circuit of the main hall. The male judge, who is flowers, is clearly well known because he is doing his own circuit of the kitchen and scrutineers' room, greeting people and cracking jokes and accepting a cup of tea. The third judge, who is domestics and has the added expertise of being head of domestic science at a girls' school, is unpacking a bag of 'instruments': knives, forks, spoons and glasses for cutting, prodding and tasting.

Madam Judge comes back for a coffee, businesslike, brisk and sensible. She says: 'The standard this year looks high, though I am always surprised at how many people get little things wrong. In runner beans one person has put in eight pods and another has put in ten and the schedule clearly says nine so they will both have to be disqualified.'

Oh, no. I was in such a hurry to put out my raspberries that I didn't count them. Go over and check. 'Damn!' There are only twelve berries on the plate and the schedule says fifteen. Sidle into the side room where I left my basket and retrieve the carton of raspberries. 'Is this cheating?' I ask myself as I put out another three. 'No,' I answer. 'The judging hasn't started yet.' Then why am I looking furtively over my shoulder and behaving like a shoplifter in reverse?

Rejoin the main group as the Hon. Sec. looks at his watch and says: 'We're running a bit late, so I think we should make a start now.' I am carrying sheets of peel-off labels and my job is to attach first-, second- or third-prize labels to exhibitors' cards when the judge has made her choice, and Sailor's job is to hurry back to the scrutineers with those results. She stops before the first class, a collection of four distinct kinds of vegetable. This is a popular class, with fourteen entries, because it attracts a high score. Each winning entry is awarded points as well as a place.

The exhibitors have their points totted up by the scrutineers and become eligible for additional prizes in the sections and in the show overall.

Most of the entries are a permutation on potato, carrot, parsnip, onion, leek and beetroot, though some also have a cabbage or cauliflower. Madam Judge glances at each entry and quickly selects the three she most likes. She lifts each vegetable, feeling for firmness and texture, sniffs them and looks for blemishes hidden on the underside. She replaces them and stands back and tilts her head and squints. Then she quickly scribbles her selection and moves on. Sailor and I have stood back deferentially during this process like courtiers to a queen, and now we step forward sharply to do the business. If we are not quick enough, she could judge the next class and be off before we are done with this one and we will miss a result, which would be disastrous.

There are several classes of onions, divided between those which weigh fewer than 8 ounces and those which weigh more. 'Scales,' she orders without looking at us, and Sailor scurries off to collect a set of brass scales. She weighs every onion, which takes a long time, and gives a little snort of satisfaction each time an onion fails the test, which means disqualification. As she moves on, she produces a magnifying glass to look for filled-in eelworm holes in the white potatoes and a knife to cut a pie section out of the beetroot to check the inside, though what for I don't know.

My Pink Fir Apples get a second in the coloured-potato class. Brilliant. I have broken my duck.

'Ah!' gasps Madam Judge when she sees the Birdman's parsnips. This is the first time she has shown any feeling. 'My goodness. Look at those.' She picks them up and runs her hands along them to see if they are floppy, which would be bad, though not surprising given their length. They are stiff and firm. She lays them down reverentially. Not only do they get first prize, she opens her bag and takes out a red sticker which reads 'Judge's Special Commendation' and puts it on the Birdman's card.

I have been sneaking glances at the other two groups and wishing I was with them because they are more relaxed, with the judges and stewards chatting away to each other and laughing. But now, as we move on to the runner beans and she bends and snaps them, Madam Judge thaws a little and starts to drop the odd comment. 'People really should read the rules,' she says as she writes N.A.S. – for Not As Stated (On The Schedule) – on the cards of the disqualified exhibits. 'They've gone to all the trouble to grow good beans, then wasted it by not counting correctly.'

There are some magnificent beans and I am not expecting to do well here. As expected I put the First label on Five Pints's card, then find myself putting Second on my own, and then Third on my purple Viola Cornettis in the French-bean class. This is exciting. I want to ask Madam Judge what was so good about them, but she hasn't thawed out that much, and anyway my heart leaps into my mouth as I see her examining my garlic and comparing it with the competition.

She picks them up and puts them down and picks them up again, as if she cannot make up her mind. I close my eyes, unable to endure the tension any more. Sailor nudges me and smiles. Yes! A First. And what's more, I have beaten Saleem, who has taken Second. I want to give Madam Judge a hug, but fear she may disqualify me for behaving Not As Stated. It was the last class in our section, and what a way to end.

The Domestic Judge has got stuck in the middle of the wine and beer classes and is giggling. She appeals to the stewards for help in choosing the winners, pleading inexperience with home-made wine and a light head after sampling a dozen bottles. 'She should be spitting it out instead of swallowing it,' says Sailor, shaking his head. Everyone crowds forward to lend a hand, not – or not only – because they are eager for a drink after a gruelling session on the judging circuit. Most of the stewards have entered beer or wine and they don't want their competitors nobbling the judge by nominating their own brews.

I sneak off to see how I did in the domestic section while the others taste and gargle and swallow and watch each other like hawks. My blackcurrant jam has won first prize for the second year running. Oh bliss. Oh joy.

Just when I think things can't get any better they do. 'Well done,' says the Hon. Sec. gruffly.

'What?' I say blankly, in the middle of studying his pickled shallots and my pickled onions and wondering why his won and mine came third.

'Your apple wine has come first and your elderflower second.' Wow! I must have died and gone to allotment heaven.

Lunch is one of the best meals I have eaten and, with twenty-odd people who share a common purpose and the glow of a tough job successfully completed, some of the best company. Everything on the table, apart from the roast meat, has been grown on the allotments. Jugs of wine and beer pass up and down and Madam Judge starts to glow pinkly and smile at everyone, and my conscience pushes me to own up about the raspberries.

'Where did I place them?' she says.

'Third. Out of a class of three.'

'In that case, I don't think any harm was done.'

At 4 o'clock the outside doors are opened for the prizegiving and the hall quickly fills. It is a real occasion and everyone has taken the trouble to dress up. It is strange to see people in suits and summer dresses who for the rest of the year are always in muddy jeans and Wellington boots. Even Mad Alice has made an effort, wearing a brown tweed suit, which looks as if it belonged to her father, and a pair of trainers.

The Hon. Sec. and his wife are the top scorers with forty prizes, and Saleem and Rita are next with thirty-six. Five Pints wins thirty-five prizes, just ahead of the Birdman with thirty-four, but he is awarded Best in Show for his parsnips and presented with the President's Trophy. The Artist wins the Silver Rose Bowl for her vases of flowers.

My tally of ten prizes, including three Firsts, may be well behind theirs, but I feel I can now keep my head up in their exalted company. I sense Arthur nodding approvingly at my shoulder and, not caring if I attract startled glances, I say: 'Thanks, Arthur. I owe it all to you.'

October

Sunday

It's my first day back from holiday and I am distinctly nervous when I open the gates. It is no longer high summer but the allotment can still change rapidly almost from day to day. What can I expect after an absence of two weeks?

Mad Alice comes up the path pushing a wheelbarrow full of weeds and prunings to the rubbish dump that now sprawls over the apron where loads of manure and wood chip are dumped on a help-yourself basis. Rubbish skips used to be sited here until the council withdrew them recently to save money. It was the only service we received from the council in return for our high rents, an average of £35 per plot per year, and it has caused a lot of resentment.

'How are things, Alice?' I say cheerily. Too late I realise that this is a mistake. She takes my casual inquiry personally and launches into a catalogue of her illnesses, giving me gruesome intimate details I do not want to hear. She tells me about her 'women's troubles' and her heart and her back and her feet, going on and on without pause until I am forced to interrupt rather rudely. 'I meant, how are the allotments?'

She sits down on the barrow and starts to roll a cigarette. 'How should they be? Can't you see for yourself?' I shouldn't have worried about being rude.

'What I mean is that I've been away for a few weeks.' Brutally Frank has arrived with his own barrow, looking as melancholic as ever.

'Had a nice time, did you?' he says in a depressed voice. 'It rained all the time you were away.' He looks at me with a gloomy relish. I smile, which is not the reaction he expected, so he adds: 'The weeds are growing like mad.' My smile broadens which goads him further. 'I wouldn't be surprised if your plot is covered in grass and stuff.' My smile is now a broad grin, splitting my face in two. He and Alice exchange puzzled looks.

What they don't know is that I am suffering from green-plant deprivation. My holiday was in southern Greece, in a place where the desert meets the sea. The land was arid stone and sand, which supported a few grey-brown shrubs and little else. The sun baked the landscape into the colour of a rock cake left too long in the oven. Within days my eyes were aching for the lack of anything green to look at. By the beginning of the second week, I was persuading my boys to take me along the coast in a sailing dinghy to scan the barren hills for any sign of green. A blade of grass, a leaf, anything. There was nothing.

Brutally Frank tips up his barrow and out cascades potato tops, grass cuttings and assorted weeds in every shade of green. I want to pick the pile up and hug it. It is lovely.

My plot is not nearly as overgrown as I expected. Here and there are patches of chickweed and clover, some tall-standing thistles and half a dozen poppies, all of which need to be pulled before they go to seed or the ground will be covered in them next year. A quick survey shows that the vegetables that are still active have thrived on a bit of neglect. The beans are cropping heavily, the peas have filled out and the courgettes have pulled their usual trick of turning into large marrows while my back was turned. The radishes have grown to the size of turnips and are good only for the compost.

The main disappointment is that the wallflower and sweet william seedlings for flowering next spring have been smothered by couch grass and creeping bindweed. The sweet peas have all finished and set seeds in pods the same as culinary peas, except they are brown.

Cut a small marrow on the edge of what is now a big marrow plantation, judging by the number of leaves, pick beans and peas for supper and some Italian red lettuce that has popped up beside the rhubarb. Then just sit in the afternoon sun for half an hour and bathe my grateful eyes in greenery and the pale reds and yellows of self-sown nasturtiums which have sprung up beside the shed. Surprised by how much sooner it starts to get dark. It is also noticeably cooler than it was a few weeks ago.

Baked Marrow Medley
Take a deep casserole dish and fill with alternate layers of marrow cut into small cubes, sliced tomatoes, chopped onion and sliced celery, sprinkle with salt, pepper, crushed garlic and two pinches of sugar. Bake for nearly an hour or until tender. For a change, cover halfway through cooking with grated cheese and allow to brown and form a crust.

Monday
Confucius is measuring his biggest compost bin with a large surveyor's tape and scratching his head and measuring again, so I ask him what the trouble is.

175

'No trouble,' he says in that bright tone people use when they don't want to explain themselves. I ask how his honey did in the show, having forgotten to check it out at the time.

'It wasn't placed. They chose the filtered and refined stuff which might as well have come from a factory. They don't appreciate the real thing as nature intends, with nothing added.'

'Or taken away,' I add before I can stop myself.

'Right,' he says, taking the remark as sympathetic understanding. He nods at the bin. 'Do you think I could build that up?'

'Why not?' I reply, thinking he means 'fill it up'.

'How high? Ten feet, fifteen?'

'What?'

'The wholesaler who supplies the organic greengrocer has offered me 30 tons of onions which have gone off. It's too good an offer to miss, but where do I put them? There's no spare patch to dump them anywhere on the allotment.'

'Well, I'm sure there's a way around the problem.' Though I think if he erects a multi-storey compost bin, the allotment equivalent of Canary Wharf, the council will throw the planning-regulation book at him.

'That's not the only problem. I have to fetch the onions myself. With that.'

'Ah.' 'That' is leaning against the fence and is currently his only means of transport since the gearbox on his ancient Fiat 600 seized up. A bicycle with a home-made trailer attached to it by an angled metal bar on a universal joint. On a good day he can shift about half a hundredweight at a time in the trailer, so long as he doesn't have to go up a hill. That means . . . I fish out a pencil and a bit of paper and calculate. 'Do you know how many journeys you'll have to make?'

'Quite a lot?'

'Twelve hundred.'

'That many?' he says unhappily. I nod sadly and leave before he gets round to asking if I'll help shift them with my car. I don't want to be mean and refuse him, but when onions rot together they exude a black oily liquid which stinks and leaves stains that cannot be removed. It's a worse cargo than raw manure.

Wednesday

'None of them will go red now,' says Saleem from across the fence as I pick more beans. I was thinking to myself that the beans are really past it now. They turn 'beany' – bulging with beans – when they are still quite small, and that is always a sure sign that they are forming that clear inner skin which is hard and indigestible. In any case I am getting sick of eating them, we've had so many at home.

'What?'

'The green tomatoes. If I were you, I'd gather them all up. The nights are getting very cold now and they'll spoil if you leave them.' Rita joins him and offers me her green-tomato chutney recipe, which seems to require a lot of chilli and sugar.

Decide to leave the rest of the beans to ripen and go brown. Will collect them next month and shell for seed.

Before I start on the tomatoes, see Magic stringing up sunflower heads for the birds and ask whether the blight he was worried about ever got this far.

'No. The outbreak seemed to peter out before it got into the middle of the site. Still, better to be safe than sorry. All my tomatoes ripened quicker at home than they would have done here.'

Poppy comes over to say she has heard great things about my apple wine and I promise to bring her a bottle. Ten minutes later the Birdman asks fondly after it – I gave him a glassful from the winning bottle at the show – and I promise him one, too.

'And one for Queeny,' he says. 'She thought it was powerful good stuff.' I had better bring several down to hand out. The haulms on the Pink Fir Apples have died down and the potatoes should be lifted soon before eelworms and black slugs start to attack them. I have never let them go full-term as a main crop before, preferring to lift them as soon as possible in the summer for salads. Put a fork in the ground and pull up what looks like a single mass of nobbly potato. There turn out to be about a dozen separate tubers growing very close to each other, all large and segmented.

Fill an ice-cream carton with Autumn Bliss raspberries, and half fill another one with blackberries. The loganberries have failed this year, probably worn out with old age. There were three vigorous plants along one of the fences when I took on the allotment and they produced a lot of fruit. Picking it required careful timing. They were a crimson red, and sour, for weeks before darkening to purple and turning sweet. Then they started to shrivel within a day or two and became chewy. The crop has been steadily diminishing for the last three years. As my attempt to rejuvenate one of the plants by layering was a failure, I think I should grub them all up and replant with tayberries or blueberries.

Friday

Drop into the Fox and Ferret after supper and discover that a special allotment committee meeting is taking place in an upstairs room to discuss vandalism and thefts. Several members adjourn to the lounge bar soon after I arrive, led by the Hon. Sec. There have been more shed break-ins while I have been away and the committee is trying to get the council to put up new security fencing where the footpath runs alongside the site.

'They are just not interested,' says the Hon. Sec. 'It would cost too much money.' As I am already at the bar when they arrive I offer them a drink, and as more and more members come downstairs it turns into a very expensive round.

'We should stage a rent strike until they do something,' says Five Pints. 'Cheers.' He lifts his pint of cider and downs half of it in one gulp.

'I told you we can't do that,' says the Hon. Sec. 'It might give them the chance to throw us all off and sell the land for houses.'

'Is that what they want to do?' I ask. This is every allotment society's worst nightmare and it is happening more and more often as pressure for new houses increases. Many of the Victorian allotments which were originally sited on the edge of towns are now nearly in the middle of them as the towns have spread, and their land is hugely valuable as well as being in just the right place for houses. He shrugs.

Middy says: 'If fencing is too expensive, we should plant a thick prickly hedge of hawthorn and brambles. It's more environmentally sound, anyway.'

Poppy adds: 'It would give the songbirds somewhere to nest and raise their chicks where the magpies can't get them.' They all speak rather wearily, as if repeating a discussion which has already been argued out with passion upstairs, and the Hon. Sec. soon changes the subject, harking back to the show.

'Your wine did well.'

'Not as well as yours,' I reply. He won ten prizes to my two.

He modestly acknowledges the truth of this and says: 'I hope people get the message that good wine can be made from just about anything grown on an allotment. You don't need grapes. In fact, home-grown grapes hardly ever produce enough sugar to ferment a decent wine.'

'Still, it would be nice to make your own grape wine. I have always had a hankering to own a vineyard. If I can't have it in Bordeaux or Burgundy or Chianti, why not here? Chateau Allotment.' Everyone laughs at the joke. But as I walk home later I think, does it have to be a joke? The Hon. Sec. is wrong. Excellent wine is made here, in little vineyards which stretch from Suffolk through Kent and Sussex to Somerset. Some of it has beaten French and German wines in blind tastings judged by international experts, though I don't suppose it has beaten my favourites, those big Australian wines which are bursting with fruity flavour. As I pass the darkened allotments a seed germinates in my mind and takes root.

Saturday

Take the car to the gates to deliver a case of my wine. Put it down outside the Hut and go in with two bottles of the apple hidden behind my back and bring them out with a flourish and present them to Queeny. 'Oh,' she says. 'Oh, you are a darling. Here.' She sits down and rummages in her bag under the counter and produces two pots of her jam, apple and damson, and seedless raspberry. They have large, bright labels on them with an allotment logo designed by Stu on his computer. 'Have those. Fair exchange is no robbery, as my old dad used to say. Mug of tea?'

'Need you ask, Queeny?'

'That's my boy. Here.' She opens a battered biscuit tin and offers me her incomparable shortbread fingers. These ones are doubles, sandwiched together with chocolate as well as having a big dollop of it at one end.

'Mm, lovely,' I say, lifting one to my mouth.

'Ta,' says Brutally Frank, pushing past me to reach for one. The lid snaps shut and he snatches his hand back just in time. He looks at his outspread fingers to check they are all still there, and goes out of the door muttering to himself.

'Some people have no manners,' says Queeny with a shake of her head.

Carry the case up to my shed and store it inside, then go and lift the biggest marrow. The stalk is so thick that the secateurs won't cut it, nor will the pruning knife, and I have to cleave it with the spade. When I stand it on one end, the other reaches up to mid-thigh. It must weigh 25 pounds or more. The skin is coarse and scarred where it has scraped against stones as it has grown. I love courgettes but have never been a great fan of cooked marrow and am thinking the inside of this one is probably both tough and tasteless.

'That's a monster,' says Five Pints, stopping his bicycle on the Ridgeway.

'What will I do with it, though? It's too big to cook, and if you could it would feed thirty people.'

'Why don't you make marrow brandy?'

'What's that?'

He lowers his bike to the ground and comes over. 'It used to be called the countryman's brandy in the West Midlands when I was a lad. What you do is cut the stalk end off like a cap, here.' He taps a point about 3 inches down. 'Then scoop out the seeds, going all the way down to within a few inches of the other end, and be sure not to break through the skin or you've had it. You'll need a long-handled spoon, although this is so big you'll be able to get your hand into it.

'When the seeds are out, pack the cavity with brown sugar and add half a bottle of cheap brandy to give it flavouring. Replace the cap and seal it on with wax and suspend the marrow in a net in a larder or shed. It will start to ferment. After a few weeks, tap a small hole in the bottom and let the liquor drip out into a jar. A big one, because this will produce a gallon, easily.'

'What's it like?'

'Potent. Yes. Really good stuff.'

'It won't make me blind, will it?'

Five Pints laughs. 'Not if you don't drink it all at once.' He licks his lips. 'Tell you what, let me know when it's ready and I'll taste it for you. Make sure it's safe.'

'Marrow brandy, eh. Well, I'll try anything once.'

Sunday

I am lifting the potatoes, what is left of the Charlotte second earlies, which are now big baking potatoes, as well as the Pink Fir Apples, when I hit major trouble. It is late afternoon and I have just pulled a cotton sweater on over my short-sleeved shirt because it is getting cool. The low sun is shining in my eyes as I drive the fork into the ground, so I think the sudden commotion around me is a blown head of dandelion seeds flying into the air. In the same instant that I suddenly see and hear that the 'seeds' are wasps I am stung, once, twice, three, four, five times.

My God. Wasps are all around my head. A cloud of them are in close and all trying to sting me. I give a yell of fright and drop the fork and windmill my arms around my face. I remember reading that when a nest is disturbed wasps become homicidal and aim for the head, where they can do the most damage. A single sting can cause death by anaphylactic shock to people who are allergic to them, and stings on the mouth and neck are the most dangerous. I have already been stung five – no, seven – times, and multiple stings can bring on shock, even in people who are not allergic. I must get away before they kill me.

I run nearly blind because I am still waving my arms to keep the wasps away from my face and ducking my head. I cross the potato patch, almost losing my footing in the newly turned soft soil, blundering through the raspberries, snapping canes, on to the path and head for the gates and refuge in my car. I don't know it, but my panic-driven progress stops people in their tracks all the way to the gates. They think I have gone mad, or am having a fit. I can't cry for help and I can't say what is happening because I daren't open my mouth in case wasps fly into it and sting me there.

Someone has just come through the gates and is bending over with a key to lock them and I just shove him out of the way and barge through. No time to apologise or explain. The car is just the other side, and now I have to stop and search for my key. I hop up and down and weave from side to side, waving the wasps away with one hand while I find the key, open the door, jump in and slam it. And now I can open my mouth and take a great, dragging gulp of air. Wasps are hitting the glass in their fury to get at me. I have run two or three hundred yards and they have pursued me all the way. There are two inside the car. I cover my hand with the sleeve of my sweater and squash them against the dashboard.

For the first time I become aware of the pain of the stings. The backs of my hands are throbbing. I have been stung at least three times on the scalp and twice on the face. I have even been stung on the legs through the thin fabric of my summer trousers. I drive home feeling my skin crawl with real or imagined wasps, and when I get there I fall through the door tearing my clothes off to the amazement of my family. There are wasps inside my trousers and my shirt. They are even inside my pockets and shoes, and I get stung twice more in the hall standing just in my underwear and socks. The boys, realising at last what is happening, grab newspapers and start swatting.

My wife fetches calamine lotion and T.C.P. and dabs me, counting the stings. Nineteen. My heart is pounding; I am light-headed and in a lot of pain.

'Am I all right?' I keep saying to her. Am I going into shock, turning blue, having a heart attack? The oldest boy fetches me a glass of brandy and I down it in one, and gradually I steady and calm down. Then I start to shiver and shake and feel faint, and go off to bed to lie down. This is one of the most terrifying things that has ever happened to me. I keep wondering how it is that I am still alive.

Thursday

I haven't been able to go back to the allotment until today, fearing that a thousand wasps would be waiting for me. My body has come up in itchy white swellings in reaction to the stings. Hives. They are everywhere, even on the soles of my feet. The doctor has prescribed anti-histamines.

I stop beside the shed. The fork lies 10 feet away where I dropped it and wasps are coming and going from a hole in the ground beside it. How did I never realise that there was a wasp's nest there? Because despite seeing the nest in the ground on Maisie's plot, I had the fixed idea that wasps made their nests up high, in trees and attics. And because their comings and goings during the summer would have been hidden by the tall potato haulms.

Now what? Feel that this is a personal struggle between me and them and don't want to ask anyone for help. I especially don't want to risk getting stung again, which is more likely if somebody else insists on carrying out some half-baked idea for dealing with them.

Go to the garden centre and buy a packet of pesticidal smoke cones which are used for fumigating greenhouses and killing aphids. At nightfall, when wasps return to the nest and stop flying, approach the nest very cautiously with a plastic bell cloche. Light two of the cones, drop them in the entrance to the nest and ram the cloche on top and run back to the shelter of the shed. Train a torch on the cloche but it has filled with grey smoke and I can't see a thing, but can hear a furious buzzing. The smoke should go down into the nest and kill the wasps, who can't escape because of the cloche. That's the plan, anyway.

Friday

It hasn't worked. The smoke has cleared from the cloche and I count eight wasps buzzing around inside it trying to find a way out. They look very angry. It's the way they are flying, head up and tail down, as if their stingers are cocked to instantly attack anything that moves.

The Birdman and Saleem are looking at the cloche from the path, and the Birdman says, 'What have you got there?' When I explain he says, 'You should have come to me. The petrol trick would soon have sorted them out.'

Saleem says: 'If you leave wasps alone, they'll leave you alone.'

'That's the trouble,' I reply bitterly. 'They didn't.'

'I'll go and get the petrol, shall I?' asks the Birdman.

'No, no. It's O.K.,' I say quickly. 'They can't last long without food. They should start dying soon.'

'Unless they tunnel their way out and come after you,' says Saleem. The Birdman cackles.

'I don't think it's funny,' I say indignantly and retire to the shed. The stings are still painful and I feel as if I am throbbing all over. At least the anti-histamines have taken the itchiness out of the hives. I watch the wasps through the window for half an hour and there is no sign of them weakening. It's impossible for me to work anywhere on the allotment while they are there, so I go home. As I pass the Birdman's shed Molly comes to the door and gestures me in.

'Sit you down. I heard about the wasps stinging you, and I've made you some ointment to rub on to take the pain away.' She offers me a jam jar half full of a murky potion. 'It's the juice of an onion mixed with a bit of washing soda and the crushed leaves of summer savory. There's nothing better for stings.' I thank her and take it home. Dab some on the back of my left hand, where the red swelling of three stings has joined up into an angry-looking comma. Within minutes the pain has lessened. Put more ointment on and half an hour later the redness has faded to pink and the pain has gone completely.

This is brilliant. Go to the bathroom and take my clothes off and swab every sting that I can reach until the jar is empty. Molly should patent her ointment. She would make a fortune.

Saturday

The wasps are dead. The inside of the cloche is littered with their striped black and yellow bodies. Return the empty jar to Molly with lavish praise and a bottle each of apple and elderflower wine and ask the Birdman to look at the nest for me. He reaches for a can of petrol, but I ask him to dig the nest out, if he will, to make sure it is finished.

The nest is a grey, papery thing which disintegrates as it comes out of the soil. There must have been a space down there, maybe formed when I earthed up the potatoes, which the queen colonised. There is nothing alive in it and we scatter the nest over the ground where other creatures can scavenge the remains.

I say to the Birdman, 'I don't understand why wasps are still around at this time of year. I thought they were all supposed to die off in September.'

'It's global warming, isn't it. It's changing all sorts of things.'

Now I feel the allotment is mine again and I can get on with digging up the potatoes, though first I check for any further wasp activity.

Sunday

There is an awful stench coming from Confucius's plot, and several people are standing round his compost bin, some holding handkerchiefs to their noses. Instead of getting the 30 tons of onions, he has collected a thousand rotten eggs and dumped them in the bin.

The smell is like sewage and it is getting worse as more and more eggs burst with the pressure of gas inside them. There is

185

no sign of Confucius, which is just as well. He would probably be thrown into the bin by his furious neighbours. It is not just the smell that annoys them, but the fear that the eggs will attract every rat and fly for miles around.

Monday
The temperature last night dipped almost to freezing, and the dense canopy of rhubarb-sized leaves over the marrows has dramatically collapsed, like spinach that has been boiled. Even more dramatic is the sight now revealed. There are dozens and dozens of marrows still partly hidden in the bed of straw I put down months ago to deter slugs. I knew there were a lot, but not a glut of this proportion.

Start to move them home by wheelbarrow before we get a proper frost, which would wreck them. It takes ages and several trips and the barrow's single wheel develops an annoying rusty squeak.

By evening, every spare surface in the kitchen is covered in marrows and green tomatoes. I could make chutney on an industrial scale, though that would simply change the nature of the storage problem. There would be several hundred jars of chutney and no takers for it. Everyone else with a surplus of green tomatoes and marrows is also making great quantities of chutney and trying to give it away.

Perhaps we should get together and form an allotment co-operative and sell it through local shops and market stalls. We could even advertise on the Internet through our web page. Or would that be a trading enterprise that is forbidden by the local council or our own rules? Must ask the Hon. Sec.

Wednesday
The Artist has set up the easel behind her shed and is painting a row of sunflowers in various stages of decline. She admits that one of the disqualified bean entries in the show was hers. 'We'd been to a party the night before and I had such a bad hangover I couldn't see straight to count.'

Start to clear the beans by stripping the fullest pods from both French and runner to take home to finish ripening and dry off. There is a danger now not just of frost but from heavy rain, which would get into the pods and rot them. Then snip off the plants at ground level to leave the roots in the ground where they will release nitrogen as they decay. Pull up the bamboo poles and slide the bean stalks off and pile up for a bonfire. I should really dip the ends of the poles which have been in the ground into a bottle of preservative so they keep longer, but I haven't got any. Tie the poles into bundles and stack behind the shed.

I am going to try growing green manure on the ground cleared of beans and potatoes. It is a bit late in the year to start growing anything, but I have a bag of tare seeds which are supposed to be able to grow in winter, mixed with fodder radish and red clover. I broadcast the seed thickly, as I'm not going to the trouble of making a seed bed and the birds will take quite a bit.

With any luck the green manure will grow before it gets too cold and stand over winter, suppressing weed growth and protecting the soil, and I will dig it in in spring before planting the regular crops.

Friday
The first of the winter programme of lectures at the church hall is on grafting and budding fruit trees. It confirms my suspicion that this is a highly skilled art best left to the experts, from whom people like me can buy the prepared trees. Useful mainly to owners of acres of land to be turned into orchards. The Ace Cultivator circulates afterwards selling tickets to the Christmas curry party. Goodness. People are already preparing for Christmas and I am still tidying away summer.

Into the Fox and Ferret to bounce my chutney idea off the Hon. Sec. He shoots it down immediately. 'Have you any idea how many regulations the E.U. imposes on commercial foods? It would cost more to deal with the red tape than we'd ever make selling the stuff. Still, if you have any other fund-raising ideas let me know.'

'Have a pint,' says Sailor. 'It's saved you a rotten job, because you'd have been landed with making the stuff.'

'But what am I going to do with all those tomatoes and marrows?' I ask despondently. I will just have to make some chutney.

Hot Green Tomato Chutney
Finely chop a large onion and fry till soft, transfer to saucepan with a pound of tomatoes, skinned, de-seeded and chopped. Add one tablespoon of oil, half a pint of vinegar, garlic, salt and pepper, 12 oz brown sugar, a pinch of crushed cumin seed and as much chilli powder as you can stand, and simmer until the liquid is absorbed into a thick pulp – about two hours. Store in screw-top jars.

The same recipe can be used for ripe tomatoes, and the chilli is optional.

Sunday
Confide in Alan about my vineyard dream, expecting him to tell me the ground and climate are not suitable. He smiles and says, 'Why not? It's a lovely idea. I grow a white grape in the conservatory at home called Seyval which would make a nice wine.'

The clocks were changed last night as British Summer Time ended and we moved back an hour to Greenwich Mean Time. Suddenly it's getting dark in what a week ago would have been mid-afternoon. I have been wearing thick woollen sweaters for a while as it has got colder, but this is the most tangible sign that winter is coming. As I stand on the Ridgeway as dusk comes at teatime, I feel the sadness that this change of season always brings.

But I also feel the tiniest bit of relief at the prospect of having a rest from all the hard work. Load the pumpkin on to the barrow to take home for the boys to turn into something scary for Hallowe'en. The split in its side has grown wider as it has grown bigger, though luckily it hasn't let rot in.

November

There is a sharp, gusty wind from the east which is chilling and I button my jacket up to the neck and pull a cap on when I go through the gates. Wave cheerily to Alan as I pass his plot. He is kneeling among his strawberries, probably weeding or potting on the runners. He waves back rather feebly, not lifting his hand above hip level, as if absorbed in what he is doing.

Strawberries are one of my 'brown thumb' plants. They go brown and die when I try to grow them, so I no longer try. It is a great shame, not only because I love strawberries and home-grown ones taste exceptionally good, but they were the first fruit

I planted on the allotment as they were one of my father's passions. He was so eager to pass on his enthusiam that he gave me sixty plantlets before I had even turned the first spadeful of earth.

Everything that could attack them in the first year did. Mildew, mould, virus disease, aphids, slugs, wasps and birds. By the second year what was left of the bed was smothered with couch grass and bindweed, and attempts to pull the weeds out simply uprooted the strawberry plants. I doubt that I harvested 2 pounds of edible fruit that year. My father swallowed his disappointment and offered me blackcurrant bushes instead and I gratefully accepted and dug the strawberries in.

Digging is on my mind today as I inspect the plot, looking in vain for signs that the green manure is sprouting. To dig or not to dig. That is the question. Whether it's better to do it now or leave it till the spring. I always have this debate with myself at the end of the growing season, look to see what other people are doing, listen to what the experts say, and then make a decision based on how lazy or energetic I feel.

It used to be a firm gardening rule that the ground should be dug over in the autumn as soon as crops were harvested, and left exposed for winter rain and frost to break the clods down to a finer tilth. This was true of heavy clay soils, and probably still is, but light soil like mine has no clods in it that need breaking down. Now, some experts think that leaving soil exposed all winter causes damage to its structure and the loss of many valuable nutrients when heavy rain washes them down to the subsoil; they say it should be kept covered.

This can be achieved either by not digging and leaving this year's crop stubble and weeds in place; digging anyway and covering the bare soil either with a mulch of compost, or with fleece, plastic sheeting, or the allotmenteer's stand-by, old carpet; or by growing green manure to protect the soil and add humus when it is dug in in the spring. Green manure is increasingly the hands-on, eco-friendly way to look after the soil in the winter, though apparently not for me. Even when I get down on my hands and knees I can't see mine coming through. Should I leave it and hope, or dig? And what about the beds which weren't sown with tares, fodder radish and clover?

When I raise my head, I see that Alan has hardly moved, so scramble to my feet and go over. He is looking cold and pale and his hands are trembling as he presses a strawberry runner into a pot. 'Are you all right, Alan?'

He gives a little embarrassed laugh. 'I've been trying to stand up for the last ten minutes and I just can't seem to get to my feet.'

'Here, let me help you.' I put my right hand under his left arm and ease him up. He is a bit shaky, so I walk him to his apple tree where he has a bench and set him down and sit with him. 'You shouldn't overdo it; it's very cold today.'

'It's my legs. Nowadays, they don't seem to want to do what I want them to do.' He gives another little laugh.

'Would you like a cup of tea or something?'

'No, no. I'll just get off home; don't let me stop you working.' He makes no move to go, and after a moment he says with a trace of bitterness: 'Don't get old, Victor. Don't get old.'

'Let me help you as far as the gate.' We walk there together and he refuses further help. I watch him go on down the lane slowly, stooped over, unsteady but still dignified and fiercely independent. I hope he is all right.

Wednesday
The weather has changed with the season. The nights are now very cold and the morning brings mist which is reluctant to clear. Wind gusts through the dry leaves on the elder and ash trees which line the railway cutting, and the crows and magpies which live in them hunch up on their branches and croak mournfully, as if complaining to each other about the weather.

Arthur says the best exhibition sweet peas are obtained from sowings made now, so go to collect seeds from the pods which hang from the dry stalks interlaced on the trellis. I have left it too late. The pods are empty. Either the birds have eaten them or the seeds have dropped to the ground and will grow naturally next year. To be on the safe side, I will buy extra seeds and plant them in pots at home to be sure of having plenty of sweet peas next year. It would be disastrous to have none. Must sow broad beans and culinary peas at the same time.

Poppy calls me over and gives me a dozen Jerusalem artichokes. They look remarkably similar to Pink Fir Apple potatoes: long and nobbly. I haven't grown them before because peeling them for cooking is difficult and they have a reputation for being more gassy than beans and Brussels sprouts. They are also invasive, running wild like mint.

Poppy confirms the last point: 'I tried growing them in a bed surrounded by a trench but they still managed to spread, so now I grow them like that.' She has made the deepest raised bed I have seen, about 2½ feet high. It is edged with old doors to keep the soil in place and prevent the artichokes from getting out.

'Is it worth it?' I ask. It looks like a lot of work.

'Oh, yes. Artichokes are delicious to eat if you cook them like potatoes and they also make a wonderful soup. And another thing: they throw up enormous leafy stalks like bamboo, 8 or 9 feet tall, so they provide a good screen if you want to block out your neighbours, or just make a windbreak. If you don't know where to put them now, heel them in somewhere and they will keep until they start to sprout in the spring.'

Not knowing where else to put them, I bury them in the compost overflow, several barrowloads of horse manure piled against one of the bins. I need to think carefully about siting them.

The sloes on the blackthorn bushes are bigger than I've ever seen them, like small grapes, and a glossy cobalt blue. Pick a couple of pounds of the ripest. The old recipes say they should not be picked until there has been a frost, which makes them juicier. I have noticed in previous years that they start to shrivel within a few days of a sharp frost and birds, which have ignored them before, then begin to eat them. Blackbirds especially love them. It is best to pick the sloes about now, before it gets really frosty, and put them in the freezer, which serves the same purpose of making them juicy and keeps them in good condition until I am ready to make sloe gin.

November

Sloe Gin

Pick half a kilo of sloes after they have been frosted, or freeze at home, remove stalks, prick with a skewer or fork so the juices will run and put into a container like a 1-litre pickling jar. Add 6–8 oz sugar and leave for three days. Add half a teaspoon of vanilla essence and top up with inexpensive gin. Leave for three months, shaking vigorously once a week. The liquor should be strained into a clean bottle and the discarded sloes can be made into a pudding. Reputed to be an aphrodisiac.

At least sloes are something I can tuck out of the way, not like the marrows, which seem to have taken up permanent residence in the kitchen. We have gone through the A to Z of marrow cooking, such as it is. Marrow baked, braised, stuffed, covered in cheese, puréed, and made into soup – I draw the line at turning them into jam and wine – and we are now heartily sick of the taste. Still the marrow mountain fills the kitchen, and daily I am asked: 'What are we going to do with them all?' In my less lucid moments I suspect they are actually multiplying when no one is around. I shall start counting them morning and night to find out.

Thursday
I have a head cold, and when it starts to drizzle, decide to cut the day short and go home to sit by the fire with a mug of hot lemon juice and honey. The Birdman comments on my streaming nose and croaky voice that the best cure for a cold is a couple of hours' heavy digging. Tell him something unprintable, but it is lost in a sneeze and a cough. The drizzle turns into a burst of heavy rain and he pulls me into his hen house to shelter from it, only it isn't a hen house any more. He has converted it into a pigeon loft, though I have to be told what the difference is.

'I got bored with the hens,' he says. 'We don't eat them because the missus won't allow it, and as pets go they're not very exciting.' The hen house – sorry, loft – is very clean and tidy, with fresh straw in the nesting boxes and little walkways or ramps to the D-shaped openings in the wall where the pigeons come and go. It is also noticeably empty.

'Where are the pigeons?' I ask.

'Up there.' He stands in the doorway and points to the sky. The rain has stopped and patches of blue are showing through the high clouds. A flock of about twenty birds is flying round and round the allotments in a wide circle.

'What sort are they?' I ask, expecting to be told they are racing pigeon.

'Tumblers.'

'I've never heard of them.'

'They fly high up, so high that they lose consciousness from lack of oxygen and come tumbling down. They regain consciousness just before they hit the ground, and then they go up and do it all over again.'

'You're pulling my leg,' I say, though with a smile because it's a good story.

'No, honestly. Up north they are very common. Fanciers put big circular mirrors on the ground for the tumblers to aim for.' We watch the birds for a while. They are wonderfully acrobatic, circling the allotments in tight formation and flying on an up-and-down and twisting path as if they're riding an invisible Big Dipper in a funfair. They don't seem interested in flying up where the air is thin and then tumbling down.

'What have you got in there?' I say as we pass the greenhouse. The shelves are covered in seed trays and pots, and he has a new paraffin heater with two chimneys.

'I'm getting a few things started early for next year. I'm going to make a big effort to beat Five Pints in the show. There was just one point in it this year, one point. It rankles, that does.' He shakes his head and pulls a face. 'He'll have to look out next year. I've got a few tricks up my sleeve.'

I sneeze again and say I must get off home. At the moment the show seems impossibly far away, on the other side of winter, and I can't begin to think about it.

Saturday

My cold is better and I venture down to the allotment in mid-afternoon to order onion sets and seed potatoes at the Trading Hut. Rita and Saleem have the gas heater going full pelt and it is nicely warm inside and redolent with the smells of peat and straw, various dried manures and muddy Wellington boots. The only aroma which seems to be lacking is wet dog. Rita makes me a cup of tea and Saleem offers me half a cob of corn from a bag of them which came out of their freezer this morning and were recooked. It tastes as if it has just been picked, the kernels popping in the mouth with buttery corn juice.

'Good, eh?' he says, and laughs when I nod my head vigorously, my mouth too full to speak. 'Have another.' I happily accept it, and then a third one.

When I have finished I say: 'I had to scrub mine from the show. When I picked them and peeled back the skins, a lot of the kernels had shrunk or collapsed. They looked terrible, as if they were diseased.'

'That was lack of moisture. If you had soaked them for half an hour, they would have plumped up nicely. No one would have known and you wouldn't have done anything wrong anyway.'

'It would have made them taste watery, though, not like these.'

'True,' he admits with a refreshing lack of false modesty.

'I wonder why they lacked moisture when it had rained so much that day.'

'Maybe you were growing them too close together so they were robbing each other.' He starts to tell me the difference between growing sweetcorn in Trinidad and growing it in England, but Rita interrupts him to unfold a poster from a gardening magazine showing about forty varieties of potato and describing their different qualities. There are some old-fashioned ones which the shops no longer stock, and some very exotic ones which I have never heard of, like the one she points to and says: 'We're going to grow that next year. I like the idea of eating a blue potato.'

'A blue potato!' I resist the temptation to say 'Yuk'. 'I couldn't eat it. It's like white tomatoes, they don't seem right.'

'But we gave you some of our white tomatoes in September.'
'Ah, yes,' I say hastily. 'That was different because I knew where they came from.' I tried a slice and left the rest because it didn't taste right, though I wonder whether if I had tasted it unseen in a sandwich I would have reacted in the same way.

People have gathered round the table to study the poster, and Poppy says, 'I'm the same. Yellow tomatoes just look unripe to me. Why breed white aubergines when being purple is part of what they are, or should be?'

'Who would want a beetroot that wasn't red?' asks Sailor.

The Ace Cultivator taps one of the illustrations. 'Nicola. I'm growing those as a new potato for Christmas in a big tub in a sheltered spot at home.'

'That's a good idea,' the rest of us chorus.

'How do you do it?' I ask.

'It's too late to start now. You should plant them in August. I ordered seed potatoes specially from a catalogue, but I'm sure you could use tubers saved when you lift your own earlies in June and July.'

I am going to grow Charlotte yet again, but I will give Pink Fir Apple a miss next year. Instead I will try Belle de Fontenoy, a French salad potato which several people have recommended.

Poppy says, 'That is the same potato as La Ratte. It has been rebranded because people weren't buying it. The name made them think of rats.'

Rita is taking orders for 3-kilo packs of seed when Middy comes in with the news that a nearby garden centre is advertising a special offer: fill a bag with as many different varieties of potato as you want from the twenty or so it stocks, all for the same price.

'They will cost a lot more than we are charging,' says Rita, sensing her trade is about to dwindle.

'But just think of all the different potatoes you can try out at the same time to see what's best. You could go for all twenty.'

Go ahead with my order and leave, reflecting that this resurgence of interest in the humble potato is probably caused by

people getting bored with the very limited choice offered by supermarkets. The council ban on bonfires is being ignored by everyone; half a dozen are burning and the drifting smoke is aromatic with dried pea vines, bean stems, willow herb and bramble canes. It is the smell of early winter, bittersweet with the sadness of another summer over and the pleasure of achievement in the harvest gathered in and the work which went into it. It is also a smell which makes me long for crumpets toasted in front of a log fire and covered with butter and home-made jam, and I quicken my step towards the gate.

Sunday
The marrow problem has reached crisis point. Tolerance in the Osborne household has snapped. It may have something to do with the dreadful mess in the larder this morning when the marrow stuffed with sugar to produce 'brandy' burst. It must have exploded under the pressure of internal fermentation. The

floor was awash with semi-liquid marrow flesh which had turned a nasty shade of brown, and everything stored on the floor and lower shelves was splattered with gungy bits. It smelt awful, like a compost heap that has gone bad, and took ages to mop up.

The daily refrain of: 'What are we going to do with all these marrows?' has suddenly become: 'They've got to go. Now.'

How? I cannot bring myself to compost perfectly good vegetables even when I have started to detest them, and the freezer is full. Then I have a brainwave: I come up with The Marrow Run.

At dusk I fill a sack with marrows and put it over my shoulder, then, armed with a list of addresses, I set off through the suburban streets. At each address I put a marrow on the doorstep and ring the bell and hurry off before it is answered. It is not that I want to avoid explanations – these have already been made over the phone. It is the jokes I cannot face. About Father Christmas, and Oooh, What A Big One!, and Burglar Bill, the reformed thief of the children's stories who broke into houses to put things back.

After the third drop a police car cruises slowly past and the two occupants give me and the lumpy sack a beady-eyed stare. I smile back nonchalantly, which must make me look as guilty as hell because the car drives on to a mini-roundabout and turns round to come back. I duck down a narrow pedestrian alley between houses which brings me out on another street, breaking out in a cold sweat at the thought of trying to explain what I am doing to two disbelieving policemen.

When the run is complete it is an enormous relief to return to a kitchen which is back to normal.

Tuesday
Send off for next year's seed catalogues. I buy most of my seed from the Organic Gardening Catalogue, which was the only supplier I could find that offered a complete organic range when I first went organic. But I still like to see what other companies are offering. The Orgies get a 10 per cent discount for a group order to the Organic Catalogue, though I don't always remember to put mine in through them. I also buy seed on impulse when I

browse through garden centres, which all now stock organic seeds and plants. I rarely give any thought to where the plants will go, which always causes problems later.

Dig up a rhubarb crown which is growing in the wrong place, by the tool locker, with the intention of putting it where the others are, by the old compost bins. It is a job and a half. The crown is really a solid root, 5 or 6 inches thick and 18 inches deep, and it takes a lot of getting out of the ground. When I do heave it out and on to the top of the locker, I am astonished to see that couch-grass roots have penetrated it in about a dozen places. It was one thing to see couch grass go through a potato, but this root is twenty times the size and very dense, and yet the couch grass has gone through it as if it was no more subsantial than a ball of cotton wool.

I am holding the crown up as if it is the Gorgon's head and the white roots are snakes when the Manager passes and I show it to him. He looks at it in amazement. 'By heck,' he says. 'I have been gardening for forty years and I have never seen that before.'

Decide not to replant it but to show it off like a trophy. Leave it on top of the locker, from where I can lift it up to amaze passers by.

Thursday
Take a close look at the frog pond with the idea of clearing out all the dead leaves that have fallen into it and discover a dozen corpses of very large slugs in various stages of decomposition. Ugh! Have they carried out a suicide pact, and why? At the same time the three frogs which lived in the pond all summer have vanished. Have the frogs moved home in disgust at what the slugs have done, or have the slugs, which the frogs were supposed to eat, eaten the frogs and then been unable to get out of the pond? Scary thought.

Middy calls over to ask if I am going to this evening's meeting of the Orgies at the Friends' Meeting House. I'd forgotten all about it, but say 'Of course' as if I hadn't, then give myself away by asking what it's about.

'Planning next year's summer outings and things,' she says.

'Are they going to make another trip to the Roof Gardens in Kensington?'

'I don't know, but I think they are going to try for a trip to Highgrove House and Prince Charles's organic farm. Oh, and Audley End in Essex. It has a 10-acre organic kitchen garden which is run by the H.D.R.A.'

They both sound good. In the event I am late for the meeting, and it has moved on from outings to trying to breathe new life into the recruitment drive which began in the spring but has never really got anywhere. It is now urgent – the membership has fallen to forty-four, and as almost the only source of income is the £6-per-head subscription, the society's finances are looking very shaky. Everyone else has been given a job for the drive and I get the only one left: designing posters to go up in allotment trading huts, public libraries and anywhere else where we might drum up business.

The newsletter which I collect on the way out carries an advertisement from the owner of a wholefood shop seeking local suppliers of organic fruit and vegetables. Top prices paid. Hm!

Saurday
November is the best time to prune fruit trees and bushes as well as plant them. Now the leaves have fallen, I can see how congested the blackcurrants are. I haven't properly pruned them since I planted them five years ago and it shows. It is the old story – I'm frightened of cutting the wrong branches or taking off too much, and doing irreparable damage. I should book myself on to a pruning course at Wisley and deal with this phobia once and for all.

I've consulted several books and they all say cut out three or four of the oldest branches at ground level each year, plus any that are weak or criss-crossing. That's it. Simple. The line drawings make it look foolproof.

The first bush is a great tangle of branches, and I have to get down on knees and elbows to get under the canopy and close enough to the base – or stool, as it is called in this case, because blackcurrants have their branches growing directly out of the ground in a clump. As I squirm in with the secateurs I hear some sharp cracks. Back out to find that three or four branches have snapped off above me, and they are not the old ones, either. I hadn't realised how brittle the wood is. When I pick up the broken branches I see they have well-formed fruit buds for next year which makes me feel worse.

Go home to collect the tree loppers so that I can cut the branches from a distance, and put the broken branches in a milk jar full of water. If they form roots I will put them in pots of sandy compost in a sheltered spot in the garden to grow and maybe give them to the Orgies to sell on their stall at the country fair next July together with any other surplus plants. Their biggest demand this year was for flowers and herbs, which is just as well as July is really too late for planting out most vegetables, even tomatoes.

The loppers work really well and I take out the oldest and thickest branches from the bottom and trim others higher up to open the centre of the bush to let in light and air. Add the prunings to the growing bonfire pile of things which won't easily compost. When the Hon. Sec. buys the industrial shredder he keeps talking about, bonfires will be a thing of the past. Cleaner air, but much less atmospheric.

Monday
There was a hard frost last night, the first 'killing' frost of the winter, the sort which penetrates cold-frames and even sheds and slaughters any tender plants inside. A white rime covers rooftops, grass and cars well into the morning. I hadn't expected anything so severe and hadn't prepared for it. Hurry down to the plot to check the damage. The tub of geraniums by the shed door and the bank of nasturtiums have all crumpled, and the few tomato plants I haven't got round to clearing have collapsed and are hanging limply from the ties holding them to bamboo canes. Otherwise everything seems all right. Wander around to see how others have fared.

Poppy has shrunk. Then I realise she is up to her waist in a hole. It is at the bottom of her plot, between the deep bed for artichokes and a water tank against which she and Carlo have stacked the usual allotment collection of odds and ends. She is working away with a spade like a miner.

'Getting up a good sweat to keep the cold out?' I say.

'What cold?' she says, stopping work. She is wearing only a T-shirt and jeans but is glowing pinkly from her exertions. The hole is deep and wide, big enough to take the roots of a well-grown tree.

'What are you putting in here, an oak?'

'Nothing. I am taking it out. This is a compost pit. I don't know where I got the idea from, but I thought that compost put into the ground would rot much more quickly than it would in a bin or a heap. And it does, in weeks. It is surrounded by earth which keeps it warm, the earth feeds in bacteria and worms to break the compost down, and it is hidden from sight. And smell.'

'What about the hard work of excavating the pit?'

'It helps if you've got a bit of a hole in the first place, as we had, but it's not that difficult. And it's easy to dig out the finished compost because it is soft. Look at this.' She slowly raises a wooden panel beside the tank a few inches and underneath are three fat frogs, huddled together and fast asleep. 'Hibernating for the winter after getting fat on all the worms and woodlice in the pit.'

Could these be my frogs, and have the ungrateful creatures deserted me because the grub is better over here?

'As I work I fill these pots with the snails I come across.' She has three 6-inch pots full of them, probably about sixty altogether. 'Have you ever put a snail on your face? When it grips the skin it is wonderfully energising. Try it.'

I take a hasty step back and raise a hand. 'No thanks, Poppy. You know, you could go into business supplying a French restaurant. You could even sell them the garlic for the sauce.' She gives me an affronted look and I remember too late that she is a vegetarian.

'No. I release the snails on the common. Carlo says there is a family of thrushes there which eats them. It must be the only place left in the district that still has thrushes.' I read recently that snails have a homing instinct as good as a pigeon and will return home in a direct line even if they have to climb over a wall to get there. The Common is half a mile away, so any of these that survive the thrushes should be turning up back here next summer, in time to eat the lettuces.

Wednesday
There doesn't seem to be much still growing on the allotment after the frost, and I look up Arthur to see what he had still in season at this time back in 1936 to compare with me. *Jerusalem artichokes* – sort of, *broccoli* – yes, *Brussels sprouts* – yes, *cabbage* – yes, *celeriac* – no, *celery, colewarts, endive, kohl-rabi, leeks, lettuce, parsnips, spinach, turnips* – no. It makes me feel inadequate, a mere amateur.

I don't even know what colewarts are. The name is not listed in the R.H.S. Encyclopedias, of Gardening or of Plants and Flowers, nor in any of my twenty-odd books on vegetable gardening, including the Geoff Hamilton ones. Arthur explains in an earlier reference in his book that they are a type of small cabbage. They must have gone out of fashion years ago. I wonder what they were like.

The wind is from the north-west where the snow comes from, and it is cold enough and the sky threatening enough for it to start falling at any minute. Surprised to see Alan out on such a day. He is standing under his apple tree leaning on a walking stick. Now, he might know about colewarts. I get no further than asking how he is.

'Not too bad, considering. The doctor says I have to have this,' he lifts the stick and waggles it, 'to stop me falling over. My legs are a bit shaky.'

That doesn't sound good, so I say: 'Alan, wouldn't you be better off at home? It looks as if it might snow.'

'I just came up today to have a look.' He sounds sad and weary, and the hand holding the walking stick has a pronounced tremor. 'I took this plot on in 1946 when I came out of the army and married Florence. We used to bring the kids up at weekends and in summer evenings for picnics. Then the grand-children. They haven't been for a while. Not since Flo . . . not since she . . . passed on.'

There is sleet on the wind now and I step up beside him and say: 'Come on. I'll take you home.'

He delays a moment longer. 'Nearly sixty years. It's been a good plot. It's given me a lot. Look after it well.'

'Of course I will,' I say, thinking he wants me to keep an eye on it till he can start coming back in the spring. He turns and we walk together slowly down the path, the sleet cutting at our bowed faces and glittering on our coats like fish scales.

Friday

The church hall is absolutely packed for tonight's talk. I have never seen it so full. The sliding doors at the back have been opened and people are spilling out into the vestibule, where it is standing-room only. The subject of the talk is the genetic mod-ification of crops, though it has been given the more user-friendly title of 'New Crops For Old – The Gene Revolution'. It makes me think of the sales pitch of the bad wizard in Aladdin when he was trying to find the magic oil lamp with the genie inside.

What all children know is that genies, once released from their lamps – or laboratory test tubes, are not only immensely powerful but totally unpredictable and therefore very dangerous. Even worse, it is virtually impossible to bottle them up again once they start to wreak havoc. What I want to know is, have the agri-scientists remembered this?

The Hon. Sec. introduces the professor of biology giving the talk, who looks slightly alarmed at the number of people facing him. He starts with a slide of Brueghel's harvesters cutting corn. The picture is a feast of rich yellows under a blue and white sky, an image symbolising the unchanging nature of farming for all that it was painted about 450 years ago.

'I did that,' the Birdman says to me in a delighted stage whis-per which carries across the hall. 'As a boy in Ireland.' People in front turn and look at us disapprovingly. They are here on seri-ous business and have no time for idle chatter from the back.

'Scything, stooking, all by hand, though we had a steam trac-tion engine to help. Those were grand days.' There is a chorus of hissing and shushing, which sounds very like a traction engine letting off steam, and the Birdman is cowed into silence.

The professor has carried on through the interruption, so I miss his remarks on the picture. He quotes the rationale for gene technology, which is the need for more reliable and pro-ductive crops to feed the world's growing population, and illustrates it with slides of famine and destitution. He moves on to the justification by scientists for manipulating genes: that they are simply speeding up and refining a process of natural selec-tion which has always taken place anyway, and which man has helped along for thousands of years in his selective breeding of animals and plants. What he does not dwell on is the transfer in laboratories of genes between totally unrelated species which could never happen in nature and is therefore, in the most literal sense, unnatural.

The professor's conclusion is rather shocking. We have all bought and eaten genetically modified food from supermarkets for years whether we knew it or not, despite certain restrictions on their use, and do we feel any the worse for it? The implication is that G.M. foods are a fait accompli and we might as well tuck in and enjoy them.

The lights go up and there is an uneasy silence in the hall as this point sinks in.

The people around me are all sorts and manner of people who have only one thing in common: that they work the earth and tend its plants. They are not horticultural Luddites deter-mined to resist change whatever it might be, but if they feel like me, we all have another thing in common: a deep and difficult-to-express anxiety that some great violation of nature might be taking place with immense consequences.

I wait, almost holding my breath, to see if they will buy the case for genetic modification. They do not. One after another they put questions which all come down to the same thing. Is it safe? The professor says: 'G.M. foods are no safer and no more dangerous than foods are at present.' That comforts no one.

Could it lead to a B.S.E.-style catastrophe? 'That concern is understandable, but there is no indication that it would happen.'

What would the effects be on birds and animals which ate the insects deliberately poisoned by modified plants? 'A very good question. We simply don't know.'

An old chap in the front row takes the unlit pipe out of his mouth and mutters: 'Things started to go wrong when we changed from hunter-gatherers to farmers,' as if he remembers the moment from his youth. The professor replies with some asperity that there would be thin pickings if any of us tried to revert to that way of life in England.

I am just recalling the scene from the film *The Day of the Triffids* when the first of those highly developed plants pulled itself out of the ground and murderously set about the complacent humans who had mistakenly thought that they were the ones in control, when the Birdman nudges me. In subdued tones he says: 'And another thing. Did you know that they can make these plants sterile? It means we won't be able to save seed from them for the next year. That will cost us a few extra quid.' Shaking his head, he adds: 'Making everything sterile. That can't be right, can it? That's not natural.'

As the Hon. Sec. rises to propose a toast of thanks, the professor reveals that he has taken on an allotment in the past few months. 'To grow my own wholesome food.' Enough said.

At the end people are as confused and worried about G.M. foods as they were at the beginning, and deeply suspicious of the technology. I share their feelings, and yet . . . and yet . . . I wonder if we are so blinded by the potential dangers that we are rejecting the potential benefits? These could be so huge, ending famine and hunger for the first time in human history, that I think the jury should stay out while trials of G.M. crops and their evaluation continue.

December

December arrives in a bad temper, blustery, cold, rainy and overcast. This is the month of least gardening activity on the allotments when most sensible people shut their plots down until the New Year and go home. It is the only month in the vegetable timetable with no sowing programme, though some enthusiasts – and trophy-chasers – will ignore convention and sow onions, leeks and tomatoes anyway in greenhouses and cold-frames.

Activity in the soil and above it comes as near to stopping as nature gets, and I admire the tidiness that brings the gardening year and the calendar year to a close together. It reminds me of something my mother-in-law once said as she tucked into a bowl of summer fruit: that the divine orderliness which ensures that as the strawberry season ends the raspberries begin and as they end blackberries arrive was proof of the existence of God. She said it with a twinkle in her eye, though as a religious woman I am sure she believed it.

I can't shut my plot down because there is too much tidying up and maintenance to do, all the things I should have done earlier in the year instead of sitting in the sun and gossiping. There is yet another job to add to the list today: the end boards have blown off the shed roof and the wind has got under the felt and ripped it. I should fix it before it rains again, otherwise everything at the far end of the shed will be soaked. There is half a roll of felt inside, and galvanised nails and a hammer, but where? There is so much clutter in there I can hardly get through the door, and I am thinking of using that as an excuse for putting the job off when Middy comes visiting.

'Yoo-hoo!' she calls from outside. 'Are you going to the organic meeting next week?' I can't turn inside the shed so I back out, kicking the door open with a heel. The wind catches it and slams it against the wall and I can sense the screws springing from the hinges. Yet another job. Sigh.

'It's the Christmas party and . . .'. Her voice tails off as she catches the full view of my Aladdin's cave. Her face registers a sort of fascinated disgust and I suddenly see my shed through her eyes. It is a shaming moment. Like most allotmenteers, I cannot throw anything away, no matter how worn out, if there is the remotest possibility of it coming in useful eventually. But why am I keeping a sack of empty bottles, a bag of solidifed cement, plastic sheeting milky with age, broken pots, rancid fertiliser speckled with mouse droppings, a folding garden chair rusted shut, a bucket with a hole in the bottom, and the rest?

Middy makes an effort to ignore what she has seen. '. . . and, uh, they are hoping you will bring the poster along to show them.'

'Poster?'

'Yes. The one you agreed to design. You know. About recruiting new members.'

'Oh, yeah.' Damn. I'd forgotten all about it. Maybe I could pay the boys to do it for me, using one of their computer programs with whizzy graphics and drag the Orgies firmly into the twenty-first century. Some of them are still happily in the nineteenth. Shut the door on the mess. It won't close properly because it has dropped about an inch. To change the subject I say: 'What are you up to today?'

'Nothing much. Lifting potatoes for supper.'

'Really? You still have some in the ground?'

'It's the best place to store them. They stay completely fresh.'

'Aren't they being eaten by slugs and wireworms? If I leave any undug beyond September, they end up with as many holes as a colander.'

'Not a nibble. They seem resistant to all pests.'

'Tell me what type they are and I'll order some for next year.'

'Desiree, and they taste very good.' The same as Saleem. I don't grow main crops because they take up a lot of space and are not a lot better than shop-bought potatoes. It may be worth trying some to lift early like I did with the Pink Fir Apples.

Wednesday

The sweet peas I sowed last month are through. I am growing them at home in the cardboard inner tubes of lavatory rolls, as I did with sweetcorn, so there is plenty of depth for the roots to develop and they can be planted into the ground where the cardboard will quickly disintegrate without the roots being disturbed. I only hope it doesn't disintegrate before it is time to plant them out next February or March. Must remember to pinch out the growing tips when two pairs of leaves have formed. This encourages side growth, which produces better flowers than the main stem.

Heavy rain yesterday and today keeps me away from the plot, and I feel restless.

Friday

No one about this morning. A leaden sky overhead, mud under-
foot sucking at my boots and a wind which comes in sharp gusts
tugging at my jacket. Crows and magpies hunting worms
brought to the surface by the rain wait until I am almost on top
of them before they flap resentfully away. There is someone here
after all, over to the right, making funny little jerking movements
like one of those mime artistes who perform in the plaza at
Covent Garden. I don't recognise him (her?) and make a detour
to pass that plot and get a closer look. It is Chicken Tom's, but
although the person on it is still some distance away with their
back to me – and is holding up a board on a short pole – I can
tell it is not Chicken Tom. It looks like a tramp. I am trying to
decide whether to say something or just retrace my steps when
the figure jerks round and falls over.

The door of the shed opens and Chicken Tom comes out
waving a screwdriver and shouts into the wind: 'He can't hold
his drink.' At least, that's what it sounds like.

'What?'

'He's on the bloody blink.' I am deeply confused. Chicken
Tom grabs the poor, unfortunate tramp and hauls him to his
feet, where I see that he – it – is not a tramp at all but a lifelike
scarecrow with a carnival mask for a face. Chicken Tom sets it
on to a stand on the ground and explains.

'The birds ignored my scarecrow when it stood still, so I
invented a moving one. It is fixed to this pole, which is mounted
on ball bearings so that it will turn easily on the stand. The
bearing came from an old bicycle wheel. That board on top of
the pole is a sail like a wind vane to turn the scarecrow.'

'Very good,' I say in admiration.

'It is when it works properly, which is hardly ever. It either
doesn't move or it moves too quickly and overbalances. That sail
makes it top-heavy, I think. Oh, well, back to the drawing board.
I'm trying to work out how to move the arms, or get it to make
loud noises. I need something extra to scare off all the pigeons.
They've just about stripped my spring cabbages.' He lifts the

scarecrow off the stand and carries it under his arm to the shed, where he turns and says: 'When it does move suddenly, you should see the birds scatter.'

Few allotmenteers are as inventive as Chicken Tom, but he embodies the spirit of practical ingenuity that nearly all of them possess. Shipwreck one on a desert island and it would be under cultivation in no time, with a comfortable shed knocked up from flotsam and a pot of palm tea on the go.

Saturday
There is a row going on in the Trading Hut when I go in to try to cadge a cup of tea to warm up. Brutally Frank and Five Pints are complaining loudly to the Birdman that his tumbler pigeons are eating their plants and that he must either lock them into their loft or get rid of them.

'I can't lock them up,' says the Birdman. 'They need to fly.'

Brutally Frank says, 'But they don't any more, do they? They just waddle from allotment to allotment, eating everything they see.'

'All my purple-sprouting broccoli,' says Five Pints.

'They're too fat to fly,' says Frank.

'And my leeks. The ones I started off early in a frame for the show,' adds Five Pints darkly, as if to suggest the Birdman had somehow got his pigeons to target them.

'Why didn't you cover them?' asks the Birdman. 'The wild pigeons will be doing much more damage than my tumblers. They get most of their food from me.'

'To be brutally frank they are pests . . .'

'. . . And if you don't control them,' breaks in Five Pints, 'someone else will. Permanently.' He lifts an imaginary shotgun to his shoulder and pulls the trigger. The Birdman puts his hat on and goes out without saying another word, his face tight with anger.

Forego the tea and go back to continue clearing out the shed. I am sorting the contents into Utter Rubbish, Useful Rubbish and Essentials. The first lot will be burnt or binned, the last kept and the middle lot will be agonised over. Patch the roof with felt and refix the end boards. On the way home later I see Molly sitting in their greenhouse. She has a pigeon in one hand on her lap and is stroking it with the other. 'Is everything all right,' I ask. 'Only I heard the row in the Hut, about the pigeons.'

'Oh, aye,' she says with a funny little smile. 'He's away now fixing up for someone to take them. I'll keep this wee one, though. It's only got one leg. No one would have it and the poor thing would likely starve to death.'

'I'm sorry.'

'Aye. So am I.'

Monday

It is a bright, sunny day with no threat of rain, so I move all the newly classified contents of the shed out, sweep the floor and the spider webs from the corners and unroll the offcuts of lino I have fetched from home. I am putting it down to stop the draughts coming up through the gaps in the planks. When it is done, put back the Essentials, tools mostly, and sit down on a chair and marvel at the space around me. More than enough to take the Useful Rubbish, so bring that back in. Space is tighter but I can still move around without knocking things over, if I am careful. Must be firm about the Utter Rubbish and burn it, though that bucket with a hole in it could be useful for keeping things in.

Wednesday

A trench has appeared on the Birdman's plot, not as big as the Ace Cultivator's but much stranger. It runs diagonally across the allotment at a sharp angle, cutting it into two uneven and oddly shaped parts. It is almost large enough for a gas main, and far too big for runner beans. He is not around to satisfy my curiosity.

Nearby, Confucius is doing what I have just done, only on a larger scale: shifting rubbish off his plot. He tells me that people in neighbouring houses have complained that his allotment is an eyesore and the council has ordered him to get rid of the boat, the trailer, his collection of oil drums and much else. He abruptly changes the subject by scooping up a handful of soil and holding it under my nose. 'Did you know that there are more living organisms in that than there are humans on the planet?'

'Er, no.'

Thursday

After much nagging from me, the boys produce the recruitment poster just before I have to leave for the Orgies meeting. It is outrageous. A riot of adolescent graphics in violent colours, overlaid with hip text in all the typefaces they could find. I start to feel a headache coming on just looking at it.

'That might be O.K. to advertise a teenage disco, but organic gardeners are sedate people. It will be a shock to their nervous systems.'

'Go on, dad. You said it needed to attract younger people.' There's no time to argue or do anything about it now, so I take it along in a large brown envelope and hope that no one asks for it.

About twenty people have turned up, a good turnout for the Orgies, and everyone has brought home-made food for the party, but no alcoholic drinks because the Quakers don't approve. I thought of smuggling in my sloe gin disguised as a blackcurrant drink, but if discovered it would have got the society expelled from the Meeting House. There are no Christmas decorations up, so maybe the Quakers don't approve of them either.

There is home-made bread and quiche, curried vegetables and kebabs of roast vegetables, curious salads with ingredients I don't recognise, lots of chicken and jugs of elderflower cordial. For once it is possible to chat to people at length without the usual talk or slide show keeping everyone quiet. Compare notes on how things grew this year and swap tips for combating the organic gardener's greatest enemy, slugs. The president of the

213

society butts into a conversation on compost to ask me if I have brought the poster. I hum and haw in embarrassment.

'Well?' she asks, fixing me with a stern look. Middy is standing behind her. I feel six years old again, in Miss Mackenzie's study at primary school where she is demanding that I hand over the frog I put into Sally Bell's hand in the playground while she had her eyes shut. I thought I was giving her a treat – I loved Horace, that frog – but Sally's screams still echo down the years.

'Well, um, yes. But it's a bit experimental, to see if it would appeal to younger gardeners.' She holds out her hand sternly. Reluctantly I pull the envelope from my pocket, then try to put it back. 'But if you don't like it, that's fine. Don't worry. I can redo it.' She takes it from me and lifts the flap to look inside. Before she can pull the poster out I say quickly: 'I've got to be going, I'm afraid. Lovely party. See you next year.'

Saturday

Find the Birdman hammering planks together to make walls about 18 inches high above the edges of his trench. The mystery deepens. 'I give up,' I say. 'What's it for?'

'Leeks.'

'Leeks?' I must sound incredulous. He climbs out of the trench and comes over.

'If Five Pints wants leeks, I'll give him leeks. If he thinks his leeks are more precious than my tumbler pigeons, I'm going to prove him wrong. When the show comes round, I'll hit him with the biggest, fattest leeks anyone here has ever seen. I will take the President's Trophy again with these leeks and publicly humiliate him.'

'Right,' I say weakly. I feel that I have missed something important in this passionate outburst. 'Why is the trench angled like that?'

'Ah.' He taps the side of his nose and smiles his crafty smile and lowers his voice. 'Have you ever been here at dawn?'

'Certainly not.'

'You should. It's a different place then. And if you had, you would know that the sun rises over there.' He points to a gap between the distant houses which is directly in line with the end of the trench.

'At this angle, the leeks will catch the very first rays of the sun. As it rises,' he tracks the course of the sun with a pointing finger, 'they will get the maximum exposure to sunlight, which is vital if they are to grow as big as I intend.'

'Won't they be in each other's shadow for part of the time?'

'No. I have made the trench wide so that I can stagger the leeks in a wavy line, out of each other's way. Over there by the pipes I am mixing the special compost to go in the trench. It will be 4 feet deep, thanks to the planks.'

I recognise the pipes. He used them to grow his prize-winning carrots and parsnips this year. They are sections of plastic drainpipe, 3 to 5 feet long and standing on end ready to be filled with sandy soil. If I was a betting man, I would be putting all my money on the Birdman for the next show. I reckon he could book the engraver now to have his name put on the President's Trophy.

Sunday

A bitter wind is blowing from the north-west, bringing little flurries of gritty snow. There is not enough of it to settle on the ground yet, though the forecast is for more to come. The frog pond is covered in ice and it is too cold to do any work, or linger longer than necessary. Pick a cabbage and some sprouts and duck into the Hut to warm up. There is a welcoming fug in there, and also a buzz of animated conversation.

'There you are, darling,' says Queeny, gently prising my frozen fingers apart and inserting a steaming mug of tea between them. 'Have you heard?'

Before she can tell me, one of the Hut Ladies says breathlessly: 'The council is getting rid of the allotments.'

'No,' says Queeny. 'They are giving up control of them.'

'What's the difference?' asks the Hut Lady.

'Privatisation,' says Confucius. 'It means we will be able to get a proper access road, better water supplies and security fences.' Faces light up at the prospect of such improvements, then cloud with doubt. It sounds too good to be true.

'That will cost a lot. Who will pay for it?' asks Saleem.

'We will, of course,' says Sailor. 'They will put the rents up.'

'Something's going on,' mutters Brutally Frank. 'And I know what it is. The council wants to sell the land for development. It would be worth millions to them if they put houses on it. This is a roundabout way of doing it.'

'They can't do that,' says Queeny in a shocked voice. 'Can they?' No one has an answer for her.

Tuesday

Will the snow hold off long enough for me to paint the outside of the shed? Yes. It is a waterproof 'wash' rather than paint. A cheerful bright-red cedar, according to the tin, but it goes on as a nasty orange. Pray it tones down as it dries.

Wednesday

It has toned down, transforming my shed so that even from a short distance away it looks quite respectable, not the sagging, splitting wreck it really is. Put on a second coat, and then it starts to drizzle. Hope it doesn't run. Now that I have given the shed a make-over, I really must put up the greenhouse. Find the four aluminium sections which make up the base and arrange them on the ground near the shed. That is where it will go, and building it will be my first project next year.

Friday

The church hall is already heaving with people and loud with music when my wife and I arrive for the Christmas curry party. Lots of familiar figures swirling by in unfamiliar party clothes and doing unfamiliar things, like dancing. Brutally Frank is wandering about forlornly clutching a bunch of mistletoe and clearing a path through the densest throng as women vanish at the sight of him. Vats of home-made curry are bubbling in the kitchen and the smells are delicious. Someone thrusts a tumbler into my hand of the Hon. Sec.'s wine. The rose-pink colour and the smell of berries are unmistakable.

Stand for a few minutes by the kitchen counter, watching everyone laughing and enjoying themselves and catching snatches of conversation. The music changes and people get up to rock and roll, and in the middle of them the Birdman and Molly dance a slow waltz cheek to cheek as if there is no one else in the hall, while gaggles of excited children run on and off the floor. They have opened a door they shouldn't have and discovered the Hon. Sec. dressing up as Father Christmas with the help of his wife and think it's a scream. This is the culmination of a year's allotmenting and nothing could be finer. Before I can get too sentimental I am dragged away on to the dance floor.

Later, when the Hon. Sec. has finished being Father Christmas and has lost his beard to the children, I ask him about the rumour circulating among the Hut gossips that the council is giving up the allotments. 'No, they've got it all wrong,' he says. 'What we want to do is go for the self-management of the allotments, which means that we get control of the budget and decide how the money is spent. There are a lot of other plans, too. We are going to deal with the vandalism problem once and for all. Next year is going to be very exciting. Why don't you come on to the committee and help us run things?'

Much later, Brutally Frank is dancing with Mad Alice. They look sweet together, both smiling with their eyes shut.

Much, much later, I am standing in the churchyard looking up at the tower as the clock strikes one and I feel a snowflake sting my nose, and another on my cheek. Then there are lots, falling silently out of a still night.

New Year's Eve
'There you are,' says the Manager from the Ridgeway. I am digging because I can no longer stand the allotment looking so

217

scruffy and neglected under its winter weeds. I am preparing the bed that will grow onions, which I will try to plant next week.

'I've been looking for you for days.'

'I haven't been here for a while because of the snow. Anything the matter?'

'I suppose you've heard the sad news about Alan.'

'What?' I feel a sudden lurch of anxiety and remember his last words to me, asking me to look after his plot. Did he have a premonition of his own death? 'What's happened? He hasn't . . . died, has he.'

'No. But he has had to give the plot up. It was too much for him. He has moved away to live with his daughter.' What a relief. Thank goodness he's all right. 'He wanted you to have the plot. Is that O.K. – can you manage it?'

I glance at it, lying beside my own and even scruffier with the remains of summer crops which haven't been cleared. The Manager takes my hesitation for doubt and adds: 'You don't have to decide immediately.'

'Yes. Yes. I'll take it.'

'Good. Alan will be pleased. He asked me to give you this.' He passes me a plastic bag and walks off. Inside is a bundle of vine cuttings and a note in spidery writing. 'Here are some cuttings from my Seyval grape to get your vineyard started. Best of luck. Alan.'

Bless you, Alan. I stick the spade in the ground and walk across to his plot and pace it out. It is roughly 17 yards each way. I do some rough calculations on the back of a seed packet. At a density of one vine per yard with a yard and a half between rows, I could put 200 plants on it, and each one when mature could produce enough grapes for between one and four bottles of wine, but call it two. That equals 400 bottles of wine.

I stare at the figure on the seed packet with excitement bordering on intoxication. My very own wine lake. Chateau Allotment.

I can imagine it now, a robust yet fragrant vintage, fruity and mellow, but best of all it would cost next to nothing after the initial outlay on vines, and I could raise many of those myself from cuttings. No tax to pay and no shipping costs. Bacchanalian romps after the harvest and the pleasure of giving bottles away to friends. Furthermore, vines require little attention apart from pruning and picking.

The Hon. Sec. was right. Next year is going to be exciting.

How To Get An Allotment

The first step is to talk to the nearest town or county hall. Local authorities, including parish councils, have a statutory obligation under the Allotment Act of 1887 to provide allotments for residents, defined as an allotted area of land let out for cultivation. If they do not have any allotments, they can be compelled to provide them under the Small Holdings and Allotments Act of 1908 if six or more residents, paying council tax or having a parliamentary vote, petition for them. Though this is a rare occurrence, a former work colleague of mine organised a successful petition in Surrey some years ago.

The attitude of councils to their allotment obligations varies enormously. Many take them seriously as a community asset. Others try to pretend they don't exist and starve them of money and support, perhaps in the hope that they will go away. Some allotment sites now occupy prime positions near town centres and a few councils regard them as a source of development land to be sold off to the highest bidder when the opportunity arises. This usually happens when a site falls into disuse, which may result from the council withholding its support.

Popular sites will have waiting lists several years long and others may be partly empty, even semi-derelict. All of them will differ greatly in the quality of the soil and available resources in the form of piped water, fencing, rubbish disposal, access for vehicles to deliver manure, trading huts supplying goods on site, and lavatories. Rents, too, can vary from as little as £5 a year to about £50. Before making a choice, it would be wise to visit all the sites in the district with vacant plots and talk to the secretary of each allotment association, as well as any plot holders willing to chat, and see what impression they make on you. Some sites are plagued by vandalism and the constant theft of tools and crops is very discouraging. Others forbid the erection of sheds; the prospect of being caught in rain storms with nowhere to shelter may be off-putting.

Allotments are also provided by self-help groups, cooperatives, charities, churches and enterprises with spare land – these include railway and water companies and some factories. Local authorities should list them. If they do not, try contacting the National Society of Allotment and Leisure Gardeners Ltd, O'Dell House, Hunters Road, Corby, Northants, NN17 5JE, telephone: 01536 266576, to which allotment societies can affiliate. It provides general guidance and information on the law governing allotments, which is complicated and often obscure, and on tenants' rights. More detailed information can be found in *The Law of Allotments* by J.F. Garner, published by Shaw and Sons Ltd, which is available in most public libraries.

It might also be worth contacting the Federation of City Farms and Community Gardens, The Greenhouse, Hereford Street, Bedminster, Bristol BS3 4NA, telephone: 0117 923 1800, which represents and advises groups converting vacant and derelict land in urban areas for cultivation.

The Henry Doubleday Research Association, National Centre for Organic Gardening, Ryton-on-Dunsmore, Coventry CV8 3LG, is Britain's biggest organic-gardening organisation. It maintains a demonstration organic allotment, and its quarterly newsletter lists vacant plots on allotment sites around the country.

One of the most exciting developments for the allotment world is the Internet revolution, which promises to bring individual associations together into national and international networks of mutual help and support. More and more allotment associations are enthusiastically signing up to the Internet and launching their own web pages, which are connected to each other in an Allotment Ring. The pages advertise plot vacancies, social outings, exchanges of seeds and plants, and annual shows. If you have access to the Internet, log on and browse. The address of my own association is: www.allotments.org